festivus

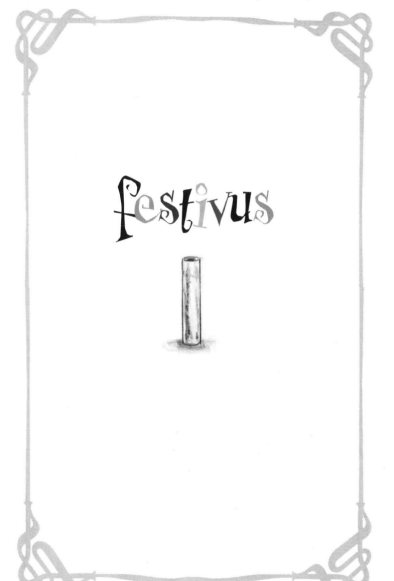

Festivus

THE HOLIDAY FOR THE REST OF US

Allen Salkin

FOREWORD BY JERRY STILLER

Illustrations by Gabi Payn

GRAND CENTRAL
PUBLISHING

NEW YORK   BOSTON

Copyright © 2005, 2008 by Allen Salkin
Foreword copyright © 2005 by Jerry Stiller

Grand Central Publishing
Hachette Book Group
237 Park Avenue
New York, NY 10017
Visit our Web site at www.HachetteBookGroupUSA.com.

Printed in the United States of America

First Edition: October 2005
Revised: October 2008
10 9 8 7 6 5 4 3 2 1

Grand Central Publishing is a division of Hachette Book Group, Inc.
The Grand Central Publishing name and logo is a trademark of Hachette Book Group, Inc.

Library of Congress Cataloging-in-Publication Data
Salkin, Allen
    Festivus : the holiday for the rest of us / Allen Salkin. —1st ed.
        p. cm.
    ISBN 978-0-446-54066-7
    1. Holiday —Humor.   I. Title.
  PN6231.H547S25 2005
  818' .607—dc22

2005015525

Cover design by Brigid Pearson

For Jay and Toby, true jokesters

Contents

foreword

BY JERRY STILLER

I n the ancient days when gods played their own games, and had their own celebrations, tossing lightning bolts between mountaintops, hurling great boulders—Festivus came out of that. It's a holiday that celebrates being alive at a time when it was hard to be alive.

There was no Christ yet, no Yahweh, no Buddha. There were great ruins and raw nature. But there was a kindling spark of hope among men. They celebrated that great thunderous storms hadn't enveloped them in the past year, that landslides hadn't destroyed them. They made wishes that their crops would grow in the fields, that they'd have food the next year and the wild animals wouldn't attack and eat them.

There's something pure about Festivus, something primal, raw in the hearts of humans.

And then there is the idea of an aluminum pole, the centerpiece of the modern celebration of Festivus.

Airplanes are made out of aluminum to take you through life from one place to another—in one piece, usually. Aluminum is a type of metal that can say so much if something is done to it, like turning it into an airplane.

But there's nothing to an aluminum pole. It has no feeling. It says, "I am what I am." You endow the aluminum pole with whatever you want to. It leaves you open to explore your own meaning. It is lightweight stuff, but in the form of an airplane it gets you from one part of the world to the next. Remember that.

And one more thing on aluminum. You don't want to put too many m's into it. "Aluminum" is easy to say, but don't think too much before you say it out loud. If you think too much about how you say it before you say it, you'll screw it up.

So with these sparks of godly and individual human imagination flying, I say this: A Festivus miracle to me would be not having to give anybody a gift during the time of year we call "the holidays," and not feeling like I've shortchanged anyone or hurt their feelings. The other end of the miracle would be that if I didn't get a gift from someone I expected it from, I wouldn't think, "Why didn't they remember me?" Nope. Just wipe the slate clean.

I mean, most of the time when you get a gift, you have to prove to the gift-giver how much you loved what they gave you. It takes a toll on you. I receive letters sometimes from people describing every little thing about the gifts I've sent to them. I don't even remember what I sent! These people should have more in their lives.

Which brings me to wrestling, another centerpiece of Festivus, the feats of strength. Wrestling is raw, primal. With my own son, I used to tumble around. He always used to come out on top for some reason. He was very agile. I let him win, of course.

Snails are primal, too. It's no coincidence there is a snail called Festivus. The snail is the ocean. Earth, wind, fire, water, the essential elements. For Festivus, make it: earth, wind, fire, and snails.

That's why if I'm to air my grievances here, I say: Let's cut this holidays thing. Let's cut it down to the bare minimum.

I am not alone in feeling this way, but very few people will actually say it out loud. Then these things like Festivus come along. Something that makes its way onto a sketch on *Seinfeld* or *Saturday Night Live* or another show like that, it comes out of something that's in the air. It resonates and people run with it.

For some people the revelation comes too late that life is best kept to the essentials. Some people are given their last rites and that person might say in their last breath, "I should have celebrated Festivus."

Look, I'm not trying to be an anticonsumer Jerry the Curmudgeon here. I'm a Gucci man, a Prada man, myself. I buy gifts from these stores. People have a right to purchase things if they want to.

All I'm saying is, if you celebrate Festivus, you may live a little longer.

You are getting back to the essentials, to the days of gods on mountaintops and howling wolves. Because you are saying the holidays are in the heart, a celebration of being alive with our fellow humans. For that purpose, an aluminum pole will do just as well as anything else—as long as it's not stuck in the wrong place.

Author's Note:

Everything in this book is 100 percent true. This is all real.

The History of Festivus

Most Festivus-friendly people believe the holiday was born December 18, 1997, the day the Festivus episode of *Seinfeld* was first broadcast. Those people are wrong.

Seinfeld, undeniably, presented this unfamiliar holiday in a seductively bitter light.

The TV version of Festivus featured a bare aluminum pole in the place of honor many families reserve for a tinsel-draped Christmas tree, an "Airing of Grievances" in which friends, family, and acquaintances accused one another of being a disappointment, and "Feats of Strength," requiring that the holiday not end until the head of the household was wrestled to the floor and pinned.

Millions of people loved it—or at least snickered at the holiday with dark pleasure. Within days of that first airing, some early adopters began celebrating their own versions of Festivus, buying poles at Home Depot, wrestling one another, and airing grievances.

Something about the holiday's anti-cheer was delivering an antidote to the tinselly, tee-hee tyranny of forced joviality that rules the modern holidays. Festivus felt right.

But despite what most *Seinfeld* watchers believed, this was not the first time Festivus had felt right to people. In various forms through the millennia, humans have celebrated holidays called Festivus. A version flourished in ancient Rome. It morphed through the Middle Ages and the Renaissance, and manifested strangely in nineteenth-century California before flowering again in upstate New York in the 1960s. What's amazing is that through its many incarnations, Festivus has always uniquely managed to express the spirit of its age just as it does now. No one has ever owned it. It is populist. It adapts. Uncontrolled by any ruling power, Festivus just grows.

Some Festivus-lovers may have a hard time believing that the holiday for the rest of us predates the twentieth century. One hopes these philistines are aware there was civilized life prior to television.

If so, let's briefly (this history lesson will end soon—but history *can* be fun. Think of those movies with revealing togas, indiscriminate conquering, and celebratory swigging from wineskins. This is like that.) travel back to the third century BCE when the Roman comic poet Plautus used the word "Festivus" to refer to wild celebrations attended by common folk. Brian A. Krostenko, an associate professor of classics at the University of Notre Dame, has studied the meaning of Festivus in the ancient world and found that even then it was something that evolved to fit its times.

Plautus, an original Festivus observer

Ancient Festivi

by Brian A. Krostenko, author of *Cicero, Catullus, and the Language of Social Performance* (University of Chicago Press, 2001)

Humans have celebrated "Festivus" for at least twenty-two centuries. In ancient Rome, *festivus* originally meant "pertaining to a festal day, a religious celebration." The word shows up in various forms according to the grammatical rules of Latin: *festivo, festivom,* and many others. For example, in the poet Plautus's *Miles Gloriosus* ("Braggart Soldier"), one character says, *"Nunc qua adsedistis caussa in festivo loco"* ("Now—to come to the reason why you've gathered here in this festal place").

For most of the year Roman society was hierarchical and restrictive, but on religious holidays—*dies festi*—people of all classes were allowed to gather and express frivolity. From this sprung uses like *festiuom facinus,* "a jolly trick" or "an impish prank" (Plautus, *Peonulus* ["Little Carthaginian"]), and the use of *festivus* as a term of endearment meaning the kind of "agreeable" one can be after a day of wine and song.

The mid–second century was a time of vast social change in the Roman republic. The social elite began throwing dinner parties like the ones they imagined the ancient Greeks had enjoyed. *Festivus* adapted, gaining a satirical spin. Thus in the (alas, fragmentary) *Menippean Satires* of M. Terentius Varrio:

omnes videmur nobis esse belli festivi, saperdae
cum simus saproi

We are jolly and jovial,
so we think.
Though in fact
we stink,
like fetid fish.

(The *saperda* was a nasty fish.) The lines parody the self-importance and would-be elegance of dinner table wits. The orator Cicero refers to a *festivum acroama,* "a delightful diversion" (*In Verrem* ["Against Verres"]), referring ironically to Verres's habit of making off with something valuable of his host's when he left a party.

As Christianity pervaded the empire, *festivus* referred not only to dinner parties and rituals in churches but also to merriments associated with pagan feast days. This ensured the continuation of the word into the Middle Ages, the Renaissance, and beyond. From *festus* was derived the Vulgar Latin *festa,* the source of Spanish *fiesta* and Old French *feste.* This was borrowed into Middle English in the form *feast* (and continued to develop in French itself, becoming *fête*). The Latin *festivus* and *festivitas* became the French *festif* and *festivité,* which in turn were borrowed into Middle English as *festive* and *festivity.*

Festivus lives.

Festivus continued to repercuss through the ages. In 1844 the word's irrepressible hold on the human subconscious manifested itself in the brain of marine biologist Richard Brinsley Hinds, who had just discovered a carnivorous sea snail off the coast of Southern California. He dubbed the snail "Festivus." The biologist is dead and no one knows why he used that name, but it was likely inspired by the creature's party-like shell, a spectacular mélange of ribbons, spikes, crests, and bulbous lumps decorated with brown stripes and flared ridges. Like Festivus's modern metamorphosis as a sharp-witted holiday, the snail has a bite—and a knack for survival. The 40- to 50-millimeter-long crustacean survives by using its razor-sharp "radula" to bore through the shells of other mollusks. "It then inserts its proboscis into the hole and sucks the other creature out and into its digestive system," says Lindsey Groves, a malacologist at the Natural History Museum of Los Angeles County. The Festivus snail spends its dozen-year life span in shallow coastal waters off Southern California and Baja.

"They leave a slime," Groves says. "That's how others of the same species find each other."

Even as a proboscis-slinging bottom-feeder, Festivus has proven irresistible. "The reason we chose it for the name of our publication, which started in 1970, was it had a double meaning," says Carole Hertz, cofounder of *The Festivus*, a scholarly journal published by the San Diego Shell Club (recent headline: "Northern Range Extension for Nuttallia nuttallii"). "It was not only the name of a species in this area but it also sounded festive."

The Festivus snail

Clearly, at the late midpoint of the twentieth century, Festivus was not merely surviving as an obscure Latin root. It was percolating, ready to be served full and steaming unto the world again. The opportunity came in 1966, when a New York intellectual named Daniel O'Keefe, who had an interest in pagan rituals and magic, was casting about for a name for a holiday to commemorate the anniversary of his first date with his wife. O'Keefe, 76 when interviewed in 2004, says the word "Festivus" just popped into his head. But with his ongoing research of ancient celebrations, it is likely the Roman use of the word was swimming around in his mind, ready to be reborn when the right occasion came calling.

As children were born into the O'Keefe household, Festivus continued to be celebrated there through the 1970s, evolving into more than the celebration of an anniversary. It gained unorthodox rituals. "There was a clock in a bag," said O'Keefe's son, also named Daniel O'Keefe, adding that he does not know what it symbolized. "Most of the Festivi had a theme," he continued. "One was, 'Is there a light at the end of the tunnel?' Another was, 'Too easily made glad?'"

As always, Festivus had arrived without dogma, a vessel that accepted what was poured into it from the hearts of the mortals who summoned it. The elder O'Keefe poured in a thick brew of the philosophy that eventually flowered into his book *Stolen Lightning: The Social Theory of Magic* (Vintage, 1983). "In the background was Durkheim's *Elementary Forms of Religious Life*," he recalled, "saying that religion is the unconscious projection of the group. And then the American philosopher Josiah Royce: Religion is the worship of the beloved community."

In other words, Festivus for the O'Keefes strived to be an expression of what was happening organically within the family's brains—not something that they were told by outside forces *should* be happening inside them.

There was no pole, but there were Airings of Grievances into a tape recorder and wrestling matches between the younger Daniel and his two brothers.

The younger Daniel grew up and became a writer on *Seinfeld*. There he appropriated and adapted the family holiday for a subplot of episode #166 (officially titled "The Strike" because of a plot involving the character Kramer's work stoppage against a bagel shop). O'Keefe the younger was the story editor on what has since become known by fans and the Festivus faithful as "The Festivus Episode." He wrote the script along with Alec Berg and Jeff Schaffer.

For *Seinfeld*, Festivus again showed it is something that can be adapted to fit anything—even the requirements of a show about nothing. On the sitcom, the character Frank Costanza tells Kramer that he invented the holiday when his children were young and he found himself in a department store tug-of-war with another Christmas shopper for a doll. "I realized there had to be a better way," Frank recounts.

The mythological birth of Festivus

A Maculate Conception:
Three Bit Players Discuss the Creation of the Seinfeld Festivus Episode

Tracy Letts is a playwright who won the 2008 Pulitzer Prize for *August: Osage County*, a play about family battles spanning generations of unhappiness and unfulfilled dreams. On *Seinfeld*, he played "Counterguy," a clerk at the off-track betting office where Elaine goes to explain she's been using their telephone number as a fake (to get rid of unwanted suitors).

Colin Malone shot to prominence in the mid-1990s in Los Angeles for his cable-access television show *Colin's Sleazy Friends*, in which he interviewed porn stars. On *Seinfeld*, he played "The Sleazy Guy," who worked behind the OTB counter assisting Counterguy. His two lines were "Elaine Benes!" and "I'm a man."

Daniel von Bargen has appeared in dozens of films and television shows, often playing a cop gone bad. He played Kruger, George Constanza's boss.

COLIN MALONE: A *Seinfeld* casting director saw *Colin's Sleazy Friends*, called me in, and gave me a part. If you're know as the guy who did the porno show, it's sort of a weird thing. But it got me in Festivus.

TRACY LETTS: The weird thing about this business is you do all these things that mean so much to you and then you work for five days on a television show and that's the thing people latch on to. People are always asking me about *Seinfeld.* I mean, Jesus, it was five days' work. Anyway, there was no studio audience that week. It was Thanksgiving week we were shooting.*

COLIN: I was leaving for the day after I did the scene at the racetrack and these two writers who were fans of my show said, "Oh, Kramer has to bring Colin with him to the Festivus party." It ment I had to work the rest of the day and it went very late and I ended up making thousands and thousands more dollars.

DANIEL: It was at the end of the week and sitting around that table as the last setup of the day, everyone was tired and had been working hard. Everybody was in a giddy mood.

TRACY: They definitely had their sh— down. They were all really talented people. This was the last season. They all knew how this stuff worked very well. Jerry Stiller is just the funniest guy I've seen in my life.

COLIN: Jerry Stiller was supposed to say Kruger couldn't do whatever his job was at all. He just kept messing it up. Everyone stared laughing. It was the only television show I was ever on that no one cared. They were just laughing. They cut out a whole sequence of him yelling at Kruger saying what a horrible person he was.

DANIEL: My memory of those things is not what you like. I don't think I've ever seen that episode. I'm not big on watching myself.

COLIN: The two writer guys said I should just sit next to Elaine. I was supposed to make Elaine uncomfortable. I was not her type. I had a line they didn't use. As they go around the table, I'm looking at Elaine and I'm drooling at her and I'm like, "You're a foxy fox." Before we shot it, Michael Richards said, "You should go up to her and say, 'You're foxy, *really* really foxy' and jump on the table and pull down your pants." I wasn't a member of SAG at the time and I was, "Dude, if I was you, maybe, but I'm not going to be rewriting dialogue and stepping on people. I'm just going to do what they tell me and hope the check clears."

COLIN: The magic of Festivus had not yet hit in my mind. In anybody's mind, really.

What Collin Malone didn't do

TRACY: My first inkling of all of this was when Ben & Jerry's came out with this Festivus ice cream. I was like, "What the hell is that?"

DANIEL: Around Christmastime, people I don't know, their humorous way of introducing themselves to me is "Happy Festivus."

*The notes on the official DVD of the episode conflict with portions of Letts's account. The DVD notes say exterior shots were shot Sunday, November 23rd, with additional shots done the next afternoon, November 24th, and the rest filmed in front of a live studio audience the following night, November 25th. The first cast reading of the script was on Thursday, November 20th. The on-screen notes also conflict with Malone's account. The notes claim that Stiller did not mess up the line, which he uttered midway through the Festivus scene during the dinner. But the notes also, confusingly, claim that at one point in the production, Stiller had been scripted to conclude the final scene at the Festivus party, where the wrestling occurs, by saying, "Happy Festivus, Georgie. This is going to hurt you more than . . . I lost my train of thought."

So Frank coined the slogan "A Festivus for the rest of us!" and formulated other rituals: The holiday occurs on December 23, features a bare aluminum pole instead of a tree, forbids tinsel, and does not end until the head of the family is wrestled to the floor and pinned. The final act of the episode shows a Festivus party at the Costanza house.

Just as the holiday changed for television—most notably with the addition of the pole—the original O'Keefe Festivus in Chappaqua, New York, was constantly in flux. "It was entirely more peculiar than on the show," the younger Mr. O'Keefe said.

On the official *Seinfeld* DVD, there is a bonus feature about the making of the Festivus episode. In it, the younger Mr. O'Keefe said his father has adjusted to the way the holiday has continued to change as it has spread into the real world. "My father's reaction to the whole Festivus phenomenon, such as it is," said the younger Mr. O'Keefe, whose shaggy hair looked soppingly overgelled for his DVD appearance, "was at first he was a little sort of weirded out by it, but evenutally it became: 'Yes! Vindication!'

"He thought his message was getting out. He was very excited by it."

Still, the elder Mr. O'Keefe's earlier trepidation reflects the knowledge gleaned from his studies of the origins of religion—that once these things start spreading, no one knows where they might go.

"Have we," he wondered when first interviewed about his holiday, "accidentally invented a cult?"

Perhaps.

The holiday has grown like mad in the real world. From a Festivus disc-golf tournament in Oregon, to a living room in Kentucky where a cat with a special "lion cut" hairdo frolics during Festivus, to a Festivus carol sung bawdily at an annual party in Manitoba, to a Festivus wine bottled on a working oil field in Oklahoma, Festivus is a gloriously fertile vine spreading everywhere. Festivus has been embroiled in a free-speech controversy in Florida, a Super Bowl victory in Baltimore, and a tax policy debate in Washington, D.C.

Festivus is just a word, and maybe that is its magic. There is no ruling force, no humans claiming otherworldly authority to dictate its rules and ordain its leaders. Festivus describes whatever it is people want to celebrate. Thanks to its star turn on *Seinfeld*, a few bare-bones rituals have become loosely attached to Festivus, but none of these are sacred. All, as is apparent throughout this book, are malleable, easily discarded in favor of something more suited to the group celebrating Festivus at any particular moment.

Something about a holiday that requires no tinsel, no trees, no dripping wax, no harvest horn o' plenty, and no flattery resonates more loudly every year. It could be that people are fed up with the commercialism of the holidays, or that there is a great yearning for an all-inclusive secular theme for December gatherings. Or it could be that Festivus is just irresistibly silly. One thing is for sure: Festivus is big. In mid-2005, there were about 118,000 Google hits for Festivus, and by 2008, there were nearly a million. Festivus has grown way beyond *Seinfeld* just as it evolved beyond what it was for the rabble of ancient Rome. It is beyond anything that can be controlled by anyone.

Preparing for the festivus Party

When Is Festivus?

For many celebrants, Festivus is not observed *instead* of the more traditional December holidays, but *in addition* to them—perhaps as an antidote to them. That's why December 23, the date for Festivus given on *Seinfeld*, is seen only as a suggestion, one that is usually ignored in favor of dates that aren't within travel periods for the more back-home holidays. Early December is popular for Festivus celebrations at offices, bars, homes, dark parking lots—anywhere.

But any day of the year can be Festivus. For the extended Kehler family, Festivus comes in July. An aluminum tent pole is erected in the center of an Ontario campground and an Airing of Grievances is held around the fire. "People tell embarrassing stories about themselves," says Therese Kehler, 40, an editor at the *Edmonton Journal*, "and kids are allowed to air grievances against their parents."

Even at the height of summer, the delicious darkness of Festivus can flourish. One year, Kehler's son expressed his disappointment about the time she didn't take him to a hockey game in which Wayne Gretzky played. Next, a female family member was ridiculed for once being so occupied flipping her hair coquettishly at a construction worker that she walked blindly into a glass door.

Therese Kehler's brother Bob topped everyone another year with his grievance against his own body, revealing a secret not even his sister had known. "He has three breasts," Therese says, explaining that she finally understood why she'd never seen her brother with his shirt off. "Three nipples."

Festivus is anytime, pretty much any way.

The Pole

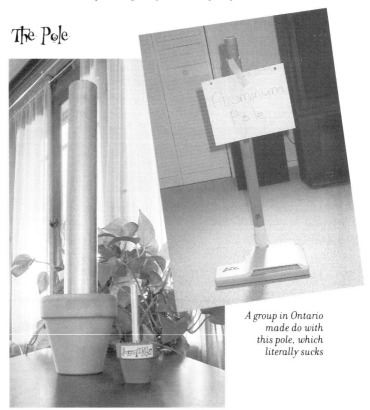

A group in Ontario made do with this pole, which literally sucks

Festivus poles can be mighty or meek, as seen in these examples from Florida

This unadorned length of lusterless metal or something that looks like metal is the one totem of Festivus that nearly everyone agrees is essential. "It has a starkness that sets it apart from the pageantry of other winter holidays," said Patrick Baker, a cryobiologist at Miami University of Ohio. "It's not telling you better days are ahead or anything else."

TYPES

Many different types of pole are used. For a party Baker attended in Oxford, Ohio, the host pried a support post from a set of steel shelves to serve as a pole and anchored it in a box filled with dumbbell weights. At financial analyst Mike Osiecki's annual Festivus in Atlanta, the aluminum fencepost he bought for $10 at a hardware store is suspended by fishing line on his porch so that "people can stare at it or dance around it if they want to."

The pole is generally metal or looks like it is metal. On the *Seinfeld* Festivus episode, the character Frank Costanza says his pole is aluminum, a substance he praises for its "very high strength-to-weight ratio." In the real world, Festivus celebrants have used cardboard tubes painted silver, aluminum foil, and heating pipes.

ACQUISITION

Poles are typically purchased at Home Depot, where a 6- to 10-foot custom cut of 2-inch-diameter aluminum electrical conduit thick enough to lever up a tipped-over Winnebago sells for about $20. A quarter-inch-diameter pole that is nearly thin enough to pick shrimp bits from a friend's teeth across the room goes for under $5. The poles can be found in the plumbing department.

eBay shoppers in December 2004 could find a "Lighted Festivus Pole, not 2B confused w/Christmas Tree" at the "Buy It Now" price of $45. The item was described as: "Hand polished Alum. Pole. Base made from MDF and hand-painted. Avail with blinking bulb or Standard Bulb. Pictures do not show the finish of this item well . . ."

Rival Amazon.com's online store featured a "Festivus Brushed Steal Pole Lamp," which looked a lot like a regular pole lamp. One customer wrote in his review of the item, "This is a pretty good, sturdy yet light enough Festivus pole to adorn your December 23rd holiday, but what's with the attached lights? I say strip 'em off."

Free, pre-owned poles are also abundant. Dumpsters outside building demolitions often hold ample lengths of used conduits, popes, and flagpoles. These items will be free, but while diving in the Dumpster, veterans advise, it is best to avoid touching anything that looks like asbestos or that has hair.

Heading to the closet has been found to solve the pole problem. By removing hanging clothes, the rod becomes available. If it's made of wood, it can be wrapped in foil. What was once obfuscated under hangers can become the star of the party.

Festivus Poles Incorporated

It is not fair to say that the most boring job in the world is manufacturing stairway railings, but let's just say it is a profession which could benefit from a little goosing up. Festivus is a world-class gooser.

One day, when Tony Leto was sitting around the offices of The Wagner Companies, a railing maker in Milwaukee, he read an article about the spread of Festivus, a holiday which requires straight lengths of aluminum.

"We make straight lengths of aluminum," Mr. Leto, the executive vice president of sales and marketing, thought. He met with his boss. "I told him," Mr. Leto recalls, " 'We're not going to make a fortune, but we're going to have fun and we get a little attention.'"

They bought the domain name festivuspoles.com. Research and development followed. A product emerged. The full-sized model, an unpolished six-foot pole with a snap-together base, was put online in October 2005 for $38. The table-top model, three-feet, sells for $30.

The governer of Wisconsin, Jim Doyle, a *Seinfeld* fan, proudly posed with his Wagner pole that year and donated it to the Wisconsin historical museum in 2006.

Blogs that mentioned Festivus started linking to the Wagner site. The Associated Press wrote about the company's poles and they appeared on *The Today Show*.

"We were getting 25 orders an hour in the days before Festivus," Mr. Leto says. "And on Festivus Eve, people were paying $200 for next day delivery."

The company sold over 1,700 poles during the 2006 season and 2,100 in 2007. Working at Wagner is now cool. Mr. Leto wishes his barber Happy Festivus.

"How much fun can there be to the aluminum railing business?" Mr. Leto asks. "This gives us something to laugh about."

The governor of Wisconsin, Jim Doyle, is almost exactly the same height as his pole.

MOUNTING

If the pole is roughly the same height as the distance between a home's floor and ceiling, it can simply be wedged between

Software consultant James Eigner salutes the pole at a party in Chicago

the two. This approach might not set the classiest mood, as exemplified by the experience of Ryan Miles, a strobe-light salesman from Nashville, Tennessee. For three Festivi (the plural of Festivus), Miles, 29, has jammed a pole between the ceiling and floor of the hallway that opens onto the den of his rented house. Of his annual party, he notes, "The guest list includes close friends and fewer and fewer girls attending each year."

(It may not only be the pole that dissuades the opposite sex. It could be the beverage of choice, a Festivus invention of Ryan and his friends called "Swill." It's made by pouring a case of beer, a fifth of vodka, and three frozen lemonade concentrates into a cooler. "The foam will settle," Ryan assures.)

There are tidier techniques. An elegant one is filling a large flowerpot with sand and working the pole into the center. Some Festivusers in Texas take the trouble to screw brackets into the floor and ceiling to hold their pole in place. Trevor Hare in Tucson worms his into a one-gallon tub filled with rocks. Unlike Ryan, Trevor exhibits class. When Festivus season passes, he says, "The pole is stored, wrapped in the finest wool, in the garage."

NOT MOUNTING

For their seven annual Festivus gatherings so far, Lianne and Mark Yarvis of Portland, Oregon, have invented their own tradition that specifies the pole must be "borrowed" and brought by a guest. A flagpole with a gold eagle on top has been among those that have served.

The pole is then passed around during the Airing of Grievances. Whosoever holds the pole must grieve. "Some people are shy about it, but if you're handed the pole it's clearly your turn," Lianne, 36, says. "It puts people on the spot. It helps break the shyness. We don't want anybody to weasel out."

TOPPING

While topping is not at all necessary, some, like Troy Kinnaird and his chums in Knoxville, Tennessee, choose to add low-key *Seinfeld*-inspired, untinselly headpieces to the pole.

Since Junior Mints, a chocolate-covered candy that in one episode of *Seinfeld* accidentally drops into a patient's body during surgery, are often served at Festivuses (another plural of Festivus), it's worth considering puncturing the candy's white cardboard box and impaling it.

Three Knoxville, Tennessee, pals who impale

AS AN APHRODISIAC

Putting a pole in the middle of a room at a party can attract strippers. At West End Comedy Theatre's 2004 Festivus celebration in Dallas, which advertised "for the nondenominational, an inoffensive get-together," female comedians took turns dancing provocatively with the pole. Party organizer Doug Ewart was stunned—and pleased. Set up under a spotlight on the comedy club's stage, "The pole saw more action than anyone else," Ewart says. "I thought it was a pretty neat development." He adds that the pole will definitely be a part of future Festivus festivities.

FOR LIMBO

While it's true that the ready availability of a metal pole can lead to some destructive party behavior (impromptu indoor baseball, apple hockey, and pretend-Superman-bend-the-rod-until-herniating not least among them), there is one primitive pole-based party activity that has lent itself perfectly to the spontaneous nature of Festivus. "My friend Dan always ends up starting a game of limbo," says Sara King, 29, a psychology graduate student who hosts an annual Festivus party in Halifax, Nova Scotia. Dan Boudreau, a medical student, is the three-years-running Festivus limbo champion of Halifax.

A warning: After limbo, the pole, now loose on the dance floor, cannot be trusted. "We used a coatrack one year," Sara says. "It got smashed all up and ended up in bed with me. I passed out and I have no idea what happened. I woke up the next morning and it was all in pieces in my bed."

Basic Rules of Festivus Limbo, Halifax-Style

Start the music (recommended: "The Limbo Rock" by Chubby Checker: "Limbo ankolim-bonee / Bend back like a limbo tree . . .").

Two players hold the pole at either end and the rest of the players form a line and try to pass under the pole without touching it.

Players cannot have any body part but their feet touching the floor.

The pole gets lowered with each round. The last player left who has not grazed aluminum is the winner.

The champion receives a shot of Sambuca. Then everyone else does shots of Sambuca, too.

NOT HAVING ONE

On the evidence, not having a pole can lead to overintellectualization of Festivus. Scott McLemee, a Washington, D.C.–based columnist for *Inside Higher Ed*, filed this piece explaining his decision to go poleless. He requests that no one leave a comment on his blog (www.mclemee.com) telling him exactly where he can stick a pole should he choose to purchase one next year.

Antidisestablishpoletarianism

by Scott McLemee

Each year, my wife and I invite friends to gather around the aluminum pole—or at least the place it would be, if we ever got around to buying one—and discuss the True Meaning of Festivus. After long cogitation, I've concluded that Festivus is the postmodern "invented tradition" par excellence.

In the premodern era, when people lived in villages, spring would draw near and everybody would think, "Time for the big party where we all eat and drink a lot and pretend for a few days not to notice each other humping like bunnies." People didn't say, "We do X because it is our tradition."

But then, starting maybe three hundred years ago, things got modern, and people started inventing traditions. In the nineteenth century folks started singing "traditional Christmas carols," even though for hundreds of years they celebrated with regular church hymns.

Postmodernism is what happens after you've been modern so long that being modern doesn't seem special. You start putting things in quotation marks—I could cite stuff here about "the decline of metanarratives" and "the simulacrum." I guess I just did.

At Festivus, all the vague hostility of enforced togetherness gets an outlet. It's hard to get sentimental about an aluminum pole, but as long as there are midwinter holidays, the spirit of Festivus will fill the air.

SOUVENIR

Guests departing from Krista Soroka's annual Festivus bash in Tampa, Florida, take with them something to remember Festivus by all year long. Here's how she does it.

Mini-Pole Party Favor

MATERIALS

plaster of Paris

container and stir stick for mixing plaster

1-inch-tall terra-cotta (also known as unglazed clay) pot

2- to 3-inch-long straight nail with a narrow (not flat)
  head

toothpick

paper

glue stick

marker

INSTRUCTIONS

Sign:

Cut a piece of paper into a rectangle that is one inch by two
inches. Fold it in half into a square. Write "Festivus Yes!
Bagels No!" so that the folded edge is on top. Rub the glue
stick on the inside of the folded paper, then fold it back over
the toothpick and seal on both sides.

Potting Mini-Pole:

Follow the directions on the plaster of Paris box for mixing
the amount of plaster you need. Pour into the pot. Quickly insert the nail into the pot (with the sharp point first so that the
party favor can't be used as a weapon if the Grievance Airing
gets out of hand) and hold it in place till the plaster dries. If
you have made a sign, insert it immediately after you insert
the nail. Hold both in place while the plaster dries.

Tinsel

Is Forbidden on Festivus. Too distracting, they say.

The tinsel industry will survive the indignity, says Marcia Ceppos, owner of the Tinsel Trading Company in New York City. "Tinsel was used going back to the 1700s," Ceppos notes. It's still used now. Designers such as Ralph Lauren, Elie Tahari, and Nanette Lepore have sewn Ceppos's tinsel into their recent clothing lines. Fly fishermen also use it to craft lures.

Anyway, sighs Steven Soprano, store manager of Holiday Tree and Trim in Bayonne, New Jersey, the increasing number of people who celebrate the holidays with artificial trees have been shunning tinsel for years. With the natural trees people used in earlier eras, tinsel gets thrown away when the dried-out tree is tossed, requiring new tinsel to be purchased every year. But with fake trees that are reused annually, one application of tinsel last forever. "You put the stuff on there," Soprano says, "it's going to be a pain to take off there."

Soprano says he's not scared of losing a few more tinsel sales to Festivus. "We may get stuck with the product," he says, "but we'll probably use it to decorate around here."

Festivus Cards

For years, there were no commercially available Festivus cards, spurring regular folk to burst forth with creative greetings and party invitations. Eventually, NobleWorks, a New Jersey-based gag card maker, had the idea to come out with a Festivus line. They used a dollop of content from the first edition of this book—and paid the author a pittance. Which is only fair since sales of the cards have only been "OK," according to NobleWorks owner Ron Kanfi. The company has done better with their other lines, such as one in which vegetables are pictured dressed up in human garb. A particular charmer shows an avocado staring at two ears of corn pictured on a computer screen. The caption: "Kevin spent the entire day downloading corn from the internet."

Hallmark has yet to weigh in on Festivus.

Homespun Festivus Greetings

The Human Fund, the Festivus Fruitcake, and Other Gifts

One of the attributes of Festivus is that there are no required gifts, no expected gifts, and, usually, no gifts at all.

On the Festivus episode of *Seinfeld*, the character George Costanza dreams up a fake charity called The Human Fund as a way to give people he doesn't care about a gift that costs him nothing. He hands office mates a card informing each that a donation has been made in his or her name to the fund. The card explains: "The Human Fund: Money for People."

Many real-world Festivites simply copy Costanza, handing out Human Fund cards. Others do give actual gifts. These have included used ChapSticks left in pockets from long-ago ski trips, balky handcuffs, and annoying talking dolls—all of which seem to establish a universal Festivus gift creed: Give only something you don't want that you expect the recipient doesn't want either.

Nothing, of course, is considered more useless and unwanted than a fruitcake. Here is a card that the operator of one Festivus Web site has developed for elevating any regular fruitcake into a Festivus Fruitcake.

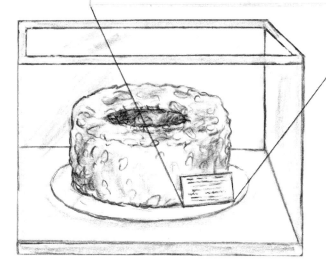

In honor of Festivus, the Festivus Fruitcake has been bestowed upon you.
You must save this fruitcake and send it to another lucky person next Festivus.
Display this Festivus Fruitcake proudly in your home.
Explain its history to those that stare in amazement at its glory.
DO NOT EAT THIS FESTIVUS FRUITCAKE!
If you consume it, you will have seven minutes of bad luck.
Leaving your mark upon it is encouraged.
Some suggestions: bronzing it, sealing it in glass, or painting it.

The Foods and Drinks of Festivus

F un, surliness, and creativity: These apparent essences of twenty-first-century Festivus are on view in what the holiday sends to the stomach. Here are some recipes developed by the Festivus-forward and details about ongoing food fights, including the nasty Beer Wars of Festivus.

Recipes

The following four recipes, created for this book, were dreamed up, styled, photographed, and described by Anna Gershenson, a caterer in Sudbury, Massachusetts, and Gabriella Gershenson, a professional food writer in New York, New York.

Shrimp Impaled on Mini Festivus Poles

Wait until a good number of guests have arrived and walk out of the kitchen carrying this while announcing the name of the dish. Stunned silence will be followed by an outburst of group glee, screams of hilarity, praises of your cleverness, and, finally, satisfied palates—because this appetizer is delicious.

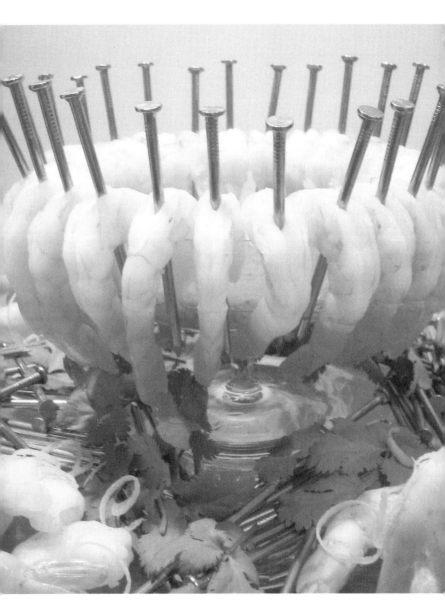

2 pounds shrimp

1 cup apricot jam

3 tablespoons horseradish

3 tablespoons whole grain mustard

2 teaspoons chili sauce with garlic

2 tablespoons lemon juice

1 teaspoon salt

2 tablespoons baking soda

20 3-inch stainless steel nails, or as many as you plan
   to use

rubbing alcohol

1. Use either good-quality frozen cooked-and-peeled
   shrimp or cook raw shrimp according to your favorite
   recipe. Chill well before serving.
2. For the dipping sauce: In a small saucepan, warm up the
   apricot jam over low heat. Stir continuously until the
   jam has thinned out.
3. Add the horseradish, mustard, and chili sauce. Stir to
   combine.
4. Remove from heat. Add the lemon juice and salt to
   taste. Serve sauce warm in a glass bowl with steep edges.

Preparing the nails:
1. Fill a pot with water 2 inches deep. Add the baking soda
   and nails. Bring to a boil. Maintain the boil for 10 minutes.
2. Remove the nails from the pot and rinse with cold
   water. Set to dry on a paper towel.
3. Moisten a fresh piece of paper towel with alcohol and
   thoroughly clean as many nails as you plan to use.

Assembling the dish:

1. Skewer the shrimp so that the top of the nail protrudes from the top of the body.
2. Place the impaled shrimp on the edge of the dip bowl, clipping them into place with the heads on the inside of the bowl and the nails on the outside.

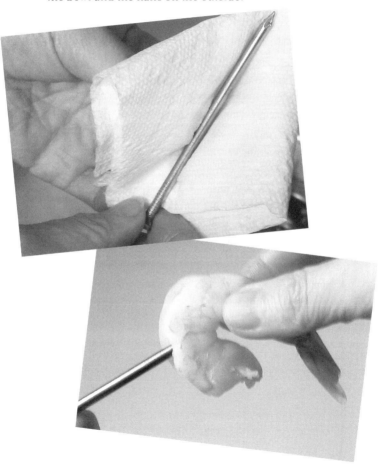

Feats of Strength Fondue with Festivus Beer

Festivus can easily be vegetarian-friendly. The nose-curling ripeness of the cheeses in this fondue will put to shame anyone who dares call vegetarians "wimps."

1 pound Emmentaler
1 pound Blue Castello or other creamy blue cheese
5 teaspoons cornstarch
1 cup hearty beer (see pp. 44–49 for where to acquire
 Festivus beer, or use a marker to write the words
 "Special Festivus Brew" below the brand name on your
 favorite can or bottle)
3 garlic cloves, finely grated
1 teaspoon grated nutmeg
1 teaspoon freshly ground white pepper
1 teaspoon water

1. Grate the Emmentaler and break the blue cheese into small chunks. Keep the cheeses separate. (Preferably on opposite sides of the room. They may start to wrestle if brought together too soon.)
2. Sprinkle 2 teaspoons of the cornstarch on each of the cheeses. Toss to coat evenly.
3. Prepare a heavy 1-quart saucepan. Pour in the beer, and add the grated garlic and spices.
4. Place the saucepan over medium heat. When the beer mixture is hot but not boiling, slowly add the cheeses,

alternating between Emmentaler and blue. Mix with a wooden spoon. Make sure to add cheese in small quantities and that it has melted before adding more. (Adding too quickly will result in lumping.)

5. Stir the mixture vigorously to achieve a smooth consistency. After all the cheese has been incorporated, dissolve the remaining 1 teaspoon of the cornstarch in 1 teaspoon water. Add to the cheese mixture, and cook together for a minute or two to bind. When it's sufficiently thick and uniform, transfer the mixture to a fondue pot.

6. Potatoes, sweet potatoes, crusty sourdough bread cubes, and string beans are fine candidates for dipping.

Ham with Junior Mint and Snapple Glaze

Not that there's anything wrong with a nice pig rump. This one, a surprisingly scrumptious and undeniably beautiful creation, is glazed with two "foods" that were used as plot devices on episodes of *Seinfeld*.

Get your ham and closely follow the instructions on the package. Forty-five minutes before the ham is done cooking, remove it from the oven to apply the glaze.

Glaze for a 5-pound ham:
1 16-ounce bottle Mango Madness Snapple
1 cup golden rum
1 cup firmly packed light brown sugar
1 teaspoon sweet paprika
1 teaspoon chili paste with garlic

32 Junior Mints, slightly crushed
1 cup strained apricot jam

1. In a heavy skillet, place all the ingredients except the
   Junior Mints and apricot jam. Bring the mixture to boil
   over high heat, mixing until the sugar is dissolved.
   Reduce heat to medium high and cook for 20 minutes
   or longer, until the mixture is reduced to the consistency of maple syrup. You will end up with about 2/3 cup.
2. Place the Junior Mints in a small heavy skillet over low
   heat. When the candies start to melt, mix with a wooden
   spoon until they form a smooth paste. At this stage, add
   the reduced syrup and apricot jam. Combine well.

Continue mixing and cooking over medium heat for another 5 to 7 minutes, until the glaze coats the spoon.

3. If you make the glaze in advance, rewarm it before applying to the ham.

Instructions for glazing:

1. Place a sheet of foil on the bottom of the roasting pan to catch run-off glaze.

2. Spoon the glaze over the ham, making sure to coat the entire surface.

3. Reapply the glaze two more times at 15-minute intervals.

Festivus Pole Stuffed with Chocolate Salami and Bitter Nibs

This sliceable aluminum "pole" pays homage to the joy that can come from pondering the bitterness of life.

4 ounces tea biscuits or plain butter cookies

2 egg yolks

1 cup sugar

1 stick unsalted butter

1 cup cocoa

2 tablespoons orange liqueur, such as Triple Sec or Grand Marnier

3 ounces ginger snaps

2 tablespoons Scharffen Berger bitter cocoa nibs

18-by-12-inch piece aluminum foil

butcher's twine, optional

1. Seal the cookies in a plastic bag and smash them with a bottle, Festivus pole stump, or a rolling pin until the pieces are no bigger than 1 inch.
2. In a bowl, vigorously mix the egg yolks with the sugar until the mixture turns thick and pale yellow. Set aside.
3. Cut the butter into 1-inch cubes and place on a cold skillet over low heat. Work the solid pieces into the melting butter with a wooden spoon or your fingers until the butter is soft but not liquid. Remove from heat.

THE FOODS AND DRINKS OF FESTIVUS

4. In a bowl, combine the egg mixture, butter, and remaining ingredients until the mixture holds shape.

5. Place the aluminum foil on a firm surface. Transfer your mixture to the foil and form a long sausage about 14 inches long and 2 inches in diameter. Place the sausage on the near end of the foil, about three inches from the edge. Roll the sausage tightly in the aluminum foil. Twist the ends of the foil as if it were a real salami. Make sure that your roll is compact and there are no air pockets. If you wish, tie the ends with butcher's twine as decoration.

6. Refrigerate for 5 hours. Slice and serve. Keep any leftovers refrigerated.

COCKTAILS

Don't Make Me Punch You Punch

Created by Julianne Donovan, host of an annual Festivus party in Kansas City, Missouri.

big bowl and ladle
fifth of light rum
2 liters ginger ale
12 limes, juiced
a few dashes of Angostura bitters
ice

Combine all the ingredients over ice in punch bowl and stir. Recommended to be served after the Airing of Grievances.

Festivus Shooters

Created by Jeremy Pollok and Eric "Bernie" Bernstrom, owners of Tonic Bar in Washington, D.C., where this was first served on December 17, 2004, as a $3 special.

1/2 can Sparks malt liquor energy drink
2 ounces cheap rum
2 ounces fruit punch
splash of Triple Sec

Combine all ingredients into a drink shaker, shake with ice, and pour into shot glasses. Makes a round of four shots.

Beer Wars of Festivus

T he three known attempts to distill the essence
of Festivus into a beer have, not surprisingly,
brewed conflict and controversy. Festivus has always
proven to have no essence to distill—except undistill-
ability. A cantankerous energy seems to result from
efforts to bottle it.

A homebrew named Festivus in a little Wisconsin
town triggered a nasty spat between local Protestants
and Catholics; in Maryland, the mere mention of
St. Festivus Ale stokes the simmering anger of its
Baltimore brewer; and in Arizona a fruity microbrew
named Festivus continues to fuel a nasty snit-fit
between the former and present owners of a troubled
Phoenix brewery.

Here are dispatches from the three battle-scarred
Festivus beer fronts.

Neenah, Wisconson—Parents at St. Gabriel
Elementary School near Appleton ignored complaints
there was something unseemly about raising money
for the Catholic school's arts program by hosting a
massive beer-drinking festival in the auditorium.

"There was some concern around the whole general idea of having this fest at the school," said Mark
Van Rossum, parent and member of Appleton Libation
enthusiasts (ALE). "But you know they also have fish
fries and bingo."

St. Festivus stands woodenly next to his Baltimore brew

The Appleton Libation Enthusiasts congregate at the birthplace of their controversial Festivus ale

ALE's entry into the homebrewfest was Festivus, a red, hoppy ale inspired by *Seinfeld* and served from an old-fashioned English beer pump engine. It was the most popular beer at the event attended by about 400 beer drinkers who paid $25 each admission. No brawls were reported at the festival.

The brawls came later.

"The Catholic church is the only church that does a lot of fund-raising with alcohol," griped Pam Garman, a Lutheran who sent a furious letter to a local newspaper after reading about the school's beer festival. "It's accepted, but that doesn't mean it's right."

Betsy Benoit, a Methodist, who, like Garman, did not have a child enrolled in the school, also wrote an angry letter. "What kind of example is that giving to our children?" she fumed.

Ruffled at the insinuations that her school might spawn a class of fifth-grade alcoholics, St. Gabriel principal Mary Jo Brown was terse. "It was a private thing," she said, refusing to comment in depth.

ALE was not so reticent.

"In Wisconsin," Van Rossum said, "its part of the lifestyle. And they got permission from the priest."

Baltimore, Maryland—During the Baltimore Ravens' 2000–2001 run through the National Football League playoffs, superstitious coach Brian

Billick forbade anyone associated with the team from using the word "playoffs." As a result, offensive lineman Edwin Mulitalo came up with an alternative name for the postseason: "Festivus Maximus."

The only problem was that two miles from Ravens Stadium, Steve Frazier and Chris Cashell, brewmasters at the Brewer's Art pub, were already serving a winter beer they'd developed two years prior and dubbed "St. Festivus Ale," a dark intoxicant with hints of bitter curaçao, orange peel, and fresh ginger.

The Ravens went on to win the Super Bowl and the word "Festivus" will live in the hearts of Baltimore's citizens forever. "It meant much more than this obscure—to some people—reference to *Seinfeld*," says Jeannine Disviscour, who curated the Festivus Maximus Super Bowl exhibition at the Maryland Historical Society in March 2001. "It was this moment for celebrating the Ravens' win and the city, the whole attempt to bring Baltimore back, Baltimore, the city that had such a high murder rate and so many challenges, that it was a citywide celebration, that this is a place people want to be and want to be a part of—we were celebrating that. That was Festivus."

All that feel-good hullabaloo angers the hell out of Frazier every time a fan tromps into his bar and praises him for naming the ale after the historic victory.

"There was no connection," Frazier spits, maintaining the he and Cashell were the first to borrow the name from *Seinfeld*, not the Ravens. Frazier continues to tap the season's St. Festivus every November—and swears it will fortify him to bash the heads of any lawyers from the Ravens or anywhere else who show up at his bar and start demanding royalties.

"Moderate drinking of St. Festivus Ale," he warns, "encourages the Airing of Grievances. Heavy drinking encourages Feats of Strength."

Pheonix, Arizona—John Watt, former owner of the Sonora Brewery in Pheonix and creator, in 2002, of a malty ale he dubbed "Festivus," believes his creation was a huge success.

"It was very well received," said Watt, who promoted the ale at a Spring Festivus '04 party (which also featured a human gyroscope ride). "It was one of our faster movers."

Watt's assistant brewer at the time, Scott Yarosh, scoffed at his old boss's memory. "It sold well in October," Yarosh said. "The rest of the year it didn't."

In 2005, Yarosh bought the brewery from Watt, who moved to Oregon where his new job is repairing automobile glass. For Yarosh, Festivus is finished. "I never really liked the name," he says. "Because of the *Seinfeld* connotations. I didn't want to get into a political thing. If someone wasn't a fan of *Seinfeld*, I didn't want them to not like my beer."

Yarosh has different ideas about how to name beers so they'll sell well. Burning Bird Pale Ale is a name he prefers over Festivus.

Watt says his former underling was always putting forth terrible marketing ideas. Killing Festivus is another one. "He's missing an opportunity," Watt says. "What's his deal?"

Yarosh doesn't care what Watt thinks. "I wouldn't," he says, "call him a friend."

Crushed Spirits

Created by a New Yorker who asked to be referred to as "Festina the Helpful Festivus Elf."

a thumb-sized piece of fresh ginger, peeled and inserted into a garlic press
crushed ice
2 ounces bourbon
4 ounces San Pellegrino Limonata (you can substitute this with sour mix and a squirt of soda)

Crush a little of the ginger into the bottom of a glass. Add the crushed ice and bourbon. If you are feeling particularly rough, it might help you to give the drink a few good shakes before you add the soda, but this is not necessary for the drink's sake.

FESTIVUS WINE

Unlike Festivus beer, Festivus wine, made in Okema, Oklahoma, has been a success. It could be that the idea of bottling wine in the town where Woody Guthrie was born pleases the "this land was made for you and me" spirit of Festivus. Or it could be that a holiday that first flourished in southern Italy prefers being accompanied by the fruit of the vine rather than the ferment of dusty grain.

"Our ranch is seven hundred acres in Oklahoma," says Jack Whiteman, co-owner of Grape Ranch. "And we have some oil and gas properties on it. We had forty acres there that was crappy sandy soil and nothing would grow, so we thought maybe we'd grow grapes on there—and darned if it didn't take off."

Because the first grapes weren't planted on the ranch until 2002, and would take years to be ready for cultivation, Whiteman got a start on building his business by buying bulk wine from California and bottling it on the ranch.

Why call the stuff Festivus?

"I was always a *Seinfeld* fan and thought it would have some marginal interest," Whiteman says. "But it has had a *lot* of interest."

First distributed in 2004, Festivus, in red, rose, and chardonnay varieties, now sells hundreds of cases annually.

Then there are the cheapskates who want their Festivus vino gratis.

"We get many 'opportunities' each year to provide wine for Festivus-related events as a 'sponsor,'" Whiteman gripes. "Usually they really are just looking for free wine." Which begs the question both freeloaders and potential paying customers may want answered: How does the stuff taste?

Okema, Oklahoma's finest vintage

A Review of Festivus Red

by Jim Clarke, wine critic for the respected Web site for culinary insiders, StarChefs.com

The Grape Ranch Festivus Red 2002 is medium ruby in color, fading to a violet-pink rim. The nose is dominated by fruity aromas and a stab of alcohol; there are clear notes of blackberry, bing cherry, and plum, while more subtle, spicy aromas of cedar and clove round out the wine. The fruit-forward character continues on the palate, while the spices broaden into touches of chocolate and vanilla. These non-fruity elements suggest the tasteful use of oak-aging. However, the only place where oak really steps forward is in the tannins; the pull of wood tannins on the cheeks is gently apparent, while grape tannins, which typically show themselves in the front of the mouth, are pretty much nonexistent.

It would make for a good cocktail wine, quite suitable to parties. Festivus Red won't overwhelm many foods; barbecue, hamburgers, and chicken dishes should get along well with it.

The wine's only serious flaw is the alcohol; as noted on the nose, there are some balance issues here. The bottle says 13.4 percent alcohol, which is fairly typical for a California red. However, while the wine is not too weighty in the mouth, the flavors do not keep pace with the alcohol in the finish, leaving instead a rather strong burning sensation in the throat.

At the Festivus Party

Stupendous Feats of Strength in Winnipeg

The Airing of Grievances

Festivus is celebrated because people want to celebrate it, not because they have to. Gushing to someone that their aluminum pole is "beautiful, a real nice pole" mocks all the times people feel social pressure to make comments like, "Nice aboveground pool, Mike," and "What a wonderful display of rat pelt coats, Marie—using them as wallpaper in the baby's room . . . wonderful!"

But such metaphorical subtlety as pole-praising is for early in the Festivus evening. Eventually most Festivus nights veer straight into the meat of the matter, the moment that

Watching other people being told what disappointments they are can be fun

never seems to come at "proper" social occasions: people telling others what they *really* think of them. This is the Airing of Grievances.

TRADITIONAL

Like everything else Festivus, the AOG has evolved some wild variations, but the core of it remains lashing into others and the world about how they have been disappointments. This usually brings participants into a circle of sorts in which each takes turns excoriating friends, enemies, relatives, acquaintances, and strangers. When all who care to have taken a turn griping, there is no required hugging or making up.

That said, it is no mere coincidence that wrestling and other fury-absorbing Feats of Strength generally follow immediately after the AOG.

NONTRADITIONAL: GRIEVANCE FRIDGES, POLE PIÑATA, AND THE ETERNAL LEDGER

There are many clever ways to castigate. There are also many stupid ways.

At Petros Kolyvas's Festivus in Montreal, a dry-erase marker is tied to the refrigerator door. The grievances are scrawled on it throughout the night and are legible until someone either rubs against the door or is thrown against it. "The fridge was instituted," says Kolyvas, a computer network consultant, "because if we did air grievances face-to-face, it might get out of hand, and people might start fighting." It is true that recent fridge grievances, such as "F——ing cell phones won't suck you off!" "Where the F—— is Krista?!"

Petros Kolyvas's fridge. early in the evening

And late in the evening

"Kelly didn't f——ing show!" and "I hate bending over," imply a level of sexual frustration that could, if uttered aloud in mixed company, lead to nose-punching.

Moving south, a group in Missouri asks everyone at their party to write down a grievance on a piece of paper and then stuff it inside the Festivus pole. At the end of the night, the pole, made of cardboard painted silver, is broken open like a piñata, papers spill out like candy, and the grievances are read aloud.

Grievance Examples

Some of these were against the world, some against enemies, some against "stupid people," and some against people's own damn selves. At Festivus gatherings around the planet, they were shouted, scrawled in dry-erase pens on refrigerators, entered into permanent ledgers, pasted on poles, and posted on Web sites.

I want this house to be decluttered—and I want you to get rid of all these ridiculous stuffed tigers!
—DOUG RUBIN TO HIS WIFE IN PRINCETON, NEW JERSEY

My brother brakes my video games.
—ANONYMOUS, NEW ORLEANS

I don't give a crap how much it sucks to be handi-capped, a $200 fine for using a handicapped spot illegally is way, way out of line.
—BILL DENNIS'S BLOG AT WWW.PEORIAPUNDIT.COM

Hoser, your girth is seriously slowing down the sponge-hockey team.
—CREG PASEHNIK, WINNIPEG, ONTARIO

I think candy canes suck, and wish that every fool that buys a cup of [coffee] . . . at $4 at pop would spill it on their laps and destroy their reproductive organs (it's my belief that stupidity is inherited).
—POST BY SOMEONE WITH THE SCREEN NAME JOE KAPPA ON THE FESTIVUS FORUM AT THE *SEINFELD* FAN WEB SITE WWW.STANTHECADDY.COM

Laura: Is "BlueMoon" really the best pseudonym you could come up with?

—WWW.TAINTEDBILL.COM

The federal government ran a record $413 billion budget deficite for the fiscal year 2004. Congress responded by passing the bloated 205 omnibus budget package that was bursting with more than 11,000 pork projects. The House of Representatives shot down budget reform with the defeat of the Spending Control Act of 2004.

—CITIZENS AGAINST GOVERNMENT WASTE ADVOCACY GROUP "TAXPAYERS CELEBRATE FESTIVUS!" PRESS RELEASE, DECEMBER 22, 2004

The Burnham Plaza Theater—your place is a dump and has been for five years.

—CHICAGOIST.COM AIRING OF GRIEVANCES. DECEMBER 23, 2004 (A COMMENT OF THIS WAS POSTED BY A "RACHELLE" LATER THAT DAY: "WE OVER AT CHICAGO METBLOG COULD TOTALLY PIN YOU CHICAGOIST WUSSIES.")

Motorists who leave top hats of snow on their car roofs are lazy. The entire sheet of snow can slide off, land on the person behind you or hit their windshield like an exploding mattress.

—MAREK FUCHS, WHO AIRED HIS FESTIVUS GRIEVANCES IN A MARCH 2005 NEW YORK TIMES PIECE "NOW IS THE WINTER OF A MALCONTENT"

"Mom, given all the time you spent ignoring me as a child, I cannot believe you still have the nerve to demand that I drive ten hours one way to eat Christmas dinner with you in a truck stop because you are too damn lazy to cook and still can't accept that I am capable of cooking the damn meal myself."
—Anonymous post on festivusbook.com, December 17, 2007

"To my throat-clearing co-worker: I hate it when you constantly clear your throat. I hate when you refuse a mint or a cough-drop. You are just an annoyance. Would you please do us all a favor and just stop? You are an inconsiderate ass . . ."
—Anonymous post on festivusbook.com, December 22, 2007

"Tara, it's espresso . . . not expresso!!!"
—Anonymous post on festivusbook.com, September 14, 2007

"People that have to ask again and again when we are going to have kids: If we are (which we aren't) it's none of your damn business! Do we want to discuss it with you? Um, no. Do we need to talk about why? No. Leave it alone!"
—Anonymous post on festivusbook.com, December 25, 2007

At Krista Soroka's bash in Tampa, a fake-leather ledger book waits on a side table. Guests approach and enter grievances in it all night long: gripes about the injustice of Ronnie getting a girlfriend, the engorged size of the New York Yankees payroll, the pathetic state of Florida's interstate road system and "the worst power grid ever." The book is kept year-round on Soroka's coffee table for visitors to mull over.

GRIEVANCES VS. FLATTERY!

Most nontraditional Airing of Grievances methods hew to the traditional idea of allowing people to unmitigatingly spew disappointment. But New Orleans, always roiling with spooky contradictions, figured out how to both celebrate and undermine the AOG.

At Festivus, The Holiday Market for the Rest of Us, first held in December 2004 on Magazine Street, attendees were invited to write grievances on slips of paper and affix them to a Festivus pole. Hundreds of people aired complaints like: "Don't call me to place an order unless you actually know what you want!" "I hate the NOPS Payroll Dept," "I singed off my eyebrows," and "Why does my roommate insist on singing opera at all times?"

SPACE TO GRIEVE

If you are not the owner of this book, please write at least one grievance on the next page about the owner. If you are the owner, write complaints about your cheap friends who, for instance, are always borrowing your books and not returning them.

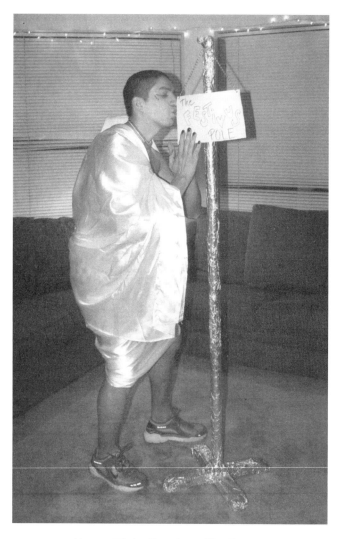

*A betogaed Carlos Almendarez of San Francisco
worships his foil-sheathed totem.*

In another homage to *Seinfeld*, the Holiday Market featured a "regifting station" where items including chipped vases and a shadow box display of golf tchotchkes were dropped off and free to anyone who wanted them. "Tags explained the history of each item," says Renee Allie, who had the paid position of Festivus Coordinator. "That stuff kept moving. The table was small and there was stuff all over it."

Among the fifty local vendors actually selling things, there was a booth from the Native American Houma tribe, where flower pins made from gar fish scales were for sale. The gar, which has a mouth lined with needlelike fangs, is like the ancient Roman saperda: nasty. So that much was within Festivus tradition.

What might not sit so well with Festivus fundamentalists (those who believe the *Seinfeld* text of Festivus is meant to be taken literally and no embellishment is allowed), was the Festivus market's Flattery Booth, held in a colorful tent named the Office of Homeland Serenity. Here, eight "Festivus Flatterers" were assigned to shower one minute of praise on anyone who requested it. "They said things like, 'You look fabulous,'" Allie says. "One flatterer played a ukulele and sang improv songs about people."

The fundamentalists can take heart. Bootlicking lost out to bitching; while about 180 people asked for flattery during the six-day event, more than 400 aired grievances.

16-YEAR-OLD KYLAH AND HER FRIENDS AIR GRIEVANCES

Kylah Eide and her friends love Festivus. They do it more than once a year. They used to gather in the Eides' living room in Timmons, Ontario, until her mother got sick of Festivus and forbade it in the house. Recent Festivi have taken place outside in the snow. They use a vacuum cleaner as their pole, the only option they can afford on their allowance-based incomes. They burn tinsel. Then they grieve. Oh how they grieve.

The Grievances My Friends and I Said to One Another

by Kylah Eide

"Courtney, you are a terrible sister. You're the dumbest one in your class and think you're better than everyone. I expected so much more than what you have become." (Courtney was about 6 years old at the time, by the way) [sister's name changed]

"When we're writing a script, you always tell everyone that you came up with my ideas."

"Your hair is disgusting."

"You wear your pants too low."

"You're terrible at basketball. Stop playing for my team."

"I've never looked at your back without seeing a thong."

"We know you lie about being a natural blond."

"You have hair sticking out of your nose."

"Your boyfriend's generally unattractive."

"I slept with your wife."

"Chris, even though you chew gum and everything, we can still smell your breath. So don't stand so close to us when you talk."

Courtney did not take it well when her sister told her she was the dumbest girl in first grade

"Stop laughing at your own jokes."

"You write bad poetry."

"We know you listen to techno."

We were starting to run out of bad things to say to each other. So we started pretending that we had other guests by doing intrepretations of them. For example, I remember telling John in my grandma's voice, "John, your pants are too long. You can't see your nice shoes!" and then making it more of a general grandmother's complaint: "I don't like Alanis Morrissette. Her hair is too stringy," and "I like Celine Dion, but she's a wretched-looking thing," and "Boys who have dreadlocks will murder you in the streets!"

Feats of Strength

As the Festivus evening progresses, human beings who have been groused at by other humans grow ornery. Orneriness begs discharge. Wrestling and other Feats of Strength deliver it.

This is natural. In olden tymes, human beings gathered nightly in public places and spent the evening talking and griping about the state of affairs until, say, a fistfight would break out. Usually no one would be seriously hurt and eventually, energy spent, everyone would go home and feel a little better about everything. These moments, which modern society has rendered scarce, are made available to humans once again through the raw expression of the collective unconscious that is Festivus.

Because fistfighting is viewed by many twenty-first-century folk as so seventh grade, Festivus devotees have tweaked the Feats of Strength in a jillion ways. There are no reported real-world cases yet of office equipment bench-pressing as an FOS variation, but, judging from the other bizarre FOS, it can't be long until Dylan from HR is on his back in the kitchenette lifting the laser printer with four reams of 20-lb., 92-bright 8.5-by-11 paper stacked on top toward the fluorescents while the entire cubicle farm stands around cheering him on and/or hoping he loses his grip and takes a nasty blow to his solar plexus.

Feats of Strength at the office Festivus party

WRESTLING

Under the *Seinfeld* orthodoxy, Festivus is not over until the head of the household is pinned to the floor. There is an undeniable classic elegance to this, especially if the wrestling match is between a father and a son. Jerry Stiller, who as Frank Costanza on *Seinfeld* wrestled his son, George Costanza (played, of course, by Jason Alexander), on the Festivus episode, notes the Shakespearean connotations in that struggle. "We were dealing with the paternalistic connection and the need to survive," he recalls. "George was the son who had gone nowhere with his life and I had to make him aware at the moment that he still had a ways to go.

"It was another kind of way with dealing with something else that was going on at the time: the rebelliousness of the son against the father and the father trying to prove he was still stronger than the son," Stiller continues. "It was like *King Lear* in Queens."

Setting the struggle in Queens changed the outcome. In the original play, the son wins. In the New York City borough, the father triumphs.

Wrestling can injure. In Tucson, Arizona, Trevor and Janet Hare threw their first annual Festivus party in December 1997 just a few days after the first-ever airing of the *Seinfeld* Festivus episode. "I wound up wrestling all my nephews," Trevor, a conservation biologist, says. "Until 1999, when I threw my back out doing it." Things at the Hare Festivus are less lumbar-intensive now. "We have impromptu arm wrestling and leg wrestling."

Less likely to cause injury—at first—is the practice of Alex

Be careful when wrestling Dad—he's crafty

Watson of Sheffield, England, whose friends square off using the *WWE Smackdown* video game. "We divide into two teams, often based on the football teams we support," he says.

In the end, though, beating the hell out of one's friends onscreen is just no substitute for leaping into actual pile drivers, body slams, eye-socket gouges, and Siberian death-locks. "It soon breaks down into a real brawl," Alex admits, "where we try and pin the members of the opposite team."

JULIANNE'S UNORTHODOX
FEATS OF STRENGTH

More civilized forms of cathartic aggression have been devised. Julianne Donovan's Festivus party in Kansas City, Missouri, flaunts a fricassee of fantastic Feats of Strength.

Most popular is the thumb-wrestling tournament, held in a leopard-spotted, red-pillared, pizza-box-sized ring. Contestants slip thumbs into tiny wrestling masks and work their hands up into the ring from underneath. Once inside the ropes, they battle until one thumb is pinned. The winner is awarded the victor's outfit, a red-and-black felt cape with a bow tie and rhinestones that fits snugly over the opposable digit that sets man apart from the beasts.

Another body-part-testing FOS at Julianne's party is the head-dunking-in-ice challenge. Whoever can keep his or her face held underwater in ice water the longest wins a pair of handcuffs. The 2004 champion made it to three minutes. "We thought he was going to pass out and die," says Julianne, a graphic designer. "It's probably good that if you try this at home, you should have someone who can resuscitate people."

It is okay to smoke cigarettes while participating in the outdoor hula-hoop contest. Not so for the indoor activity of weight-holding. Contestants hold a hand weight with one arm extended straight out. The winner is the person who holds the weight in the air longest without buckling.

The activities add spark—and cull creeps. "If you're around boring people or some obnoxious man," Julianne says, "you can say, 'Oh, there's thumb wrestling in the other room. Bye!'"

Not that hookups are frowned upon. A somewhat sugges-
tive Big Ball competition requires contestants to blow up bal-
loon punch-balls and punch them for
as long as possible without losing
control.

And then later, perhaps as a
result of releasing all this aggression, comes spin-the-bottle.
This, Julianne says of the 2004
party, resulted in an impressive
feat.

"Everyone was making out
with each other."

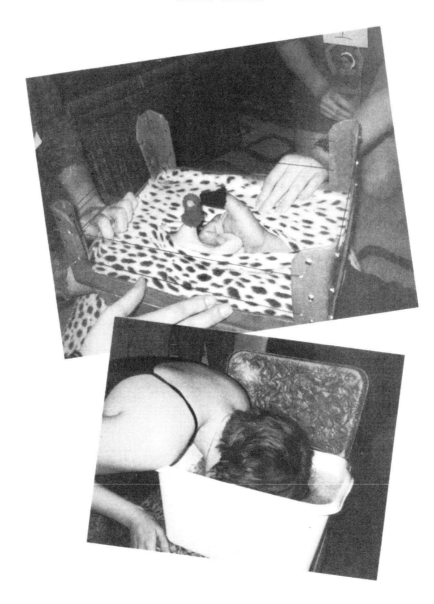

BULL RIDING

Speaking of looking for love, the hit 1980 movie *Urban Cowboy*, which featured the song "Looking for Love (In All the Wrong Places)," ushered in a trend of bars installing mechanical bulls. If the way they celebrate Festivus in Springfield, Illinois, catches on, mechanical bulls could ride high again.

In addition to the Pontani sisters' "clean burlesque" act and ample beer, the Winter Festivus Pageant held in 2004 in a Hilton ballroom featured, as its FOS challenge, a mechanical bull. (There was also, appropriately, a band called Los Straitjackets, who performed surf music wearing Mexican wrestling masks—but there was no actual wrestling, Mexican or any other kind.)

This unusual Feat of Strength helped host Wade Ebert talk

A Feat of Strength in Springfield, Illinois

a friend out of attending an office holiday party and into forking out $15 to join hundreds of others at the Festivus pageant. "I told him," Ebert recalls, "'Christ, I got a band, I got two bands, I got four Mexican wrestling masks, I got three go-go dancers, I got a mechanical bull. Why don't you bring some people from your lame Christmas party?' Guy skipped the Christmas party, came to Festivus instead."

What killed the bull fad in the 1980s was a grisly toll of broken arms and concussions. But at Ebert's Festivus, promisingly, there were no injuries.

An Unusual Distraction from the Feats of Strength: Cat with a Lion Cut

At a Festivus party in Louisville, Kentucky, guests were stunned when the host family's cat sprang into the living room with a "lion cut," its torso shorn nearly bald but the mane left full around the head and the fur long at the feet and tip of the tail. The hosts claimed they had shorn the feline in an effort to prevent dreadlocks, but guests suspected the awful primping was merely an effort to startle Festivus guests so profoundly that they'd falter during the Feats of Strength. "I found it distracting," said Lisa, a guest who asked that her last name not appear in print. "Every time the cat would come in, my friend and I would scream and point and laugh. Eventually the cat stopped coming in."

Lisa and the other guests were unlikely to do well at the Feats of Strength in any case because they were spending so much time around a four-foot-high, water-filled tobacco-smoking devise. "It was our pole," Lisa recalled. The sweet-smelling pole and the weird cat were just about all she recalled. "There might have been wrestling. I can't remember," she said. Then she started talking about the cat again. "That poor animal looked really pissed off."

Despite repeated calls, the hosts who gave the lion cut to their cat refused comment. The following photos of a different cat with a lion cut were found while researching this book, were taken long before work began on this book, and were not set up or done for this book. The author likes cats and would never lion cut one.

This, the author suggests, is unFestivuslike.

Festivus Miracles

These are basically not miracles. Like the praising of a host's bare aluminum pole, declaring that something is "a Festivus miracle!" is a smart-ass way Festivusers mock the clichés of other holidays. One such cliché is apparent every time a 6–5 college football team wins whatever lame bowl game is being played on December 25 that year, and the team's local newspaper headlines the victory a "CHRIST-MAS MIRACLE!"

Christmas and Hanukkah and other "real" holidays are supposed to commemorate real miracles, like a one-day supply of oil lasting eight days and a virgin giving birth—not a trained field goal kicker kicking a 28-yard winning field goal against another 6–5 team or an automobile company offering onetime only 1.5 percent financing on all vehicles bought from dealer stock before January 10.

In fact, a mediocre deal on car financing and a field goal kicker kicking a field goal are much more like Festivus miracles than Christmas miracles, no matter what a TV ad or a sports page blares. They're not miraculous. Just as someone's friend named Max who was invited to a Festivus party and who said he was going to show up at that Festivus party and who is known for keeping his commitments actually arriving at the party sometime around the time he said he was going to arrive is not a real miracle. It's a semipleasant or potentially unpleasant—if Max is not well-liked—reality.

Thus, when Max enters the room, Festivus custom deems it appropriate to cry out, "Max is here! It's a Festivus miracle."

If Max is not liked, it is considered best for the person who likes him least to declare the miracle. In that way, the automobile company, the 6–5 team, Max, and everything else so deserving is mocked.

New Festivus Activities

The rules of this holiday are not written in stone—or even Jell-O. There are no unbreakable rules written down at all. It is possible that there is a holiday being celebrated right now on the planet Gorzex during which elder females, for entertainment, spew regurgitated skeelg larvae onto fledderberry flowers. As long as that behavior is not absolutely required by the dictates of some higher authority, the Gorzexians are free to call the holiday Festivus as far as any Earthlings are concerned.

In fact, they can change the whole thing around and juggle ligmomarry pups (they like being juggled) on their Festivus if they want. Festivus can stand it. Can any other human holiday?

Evidence for this Gorzexian level of adaptability is found in the way humans here on Earth have molded the holiday to fit their whims.

WASHER PITCHING
For instance, the Festivus party that Katherine Willis, an actress, and her husband, Jed Thornock, a computer programmer, give in Austin, Texas, every Christmas Eve eve includes a backyard game of "pitching washers." Katherine calls it "the redneck equivalent of horseshoes."

"There's basically a hole in the ground," she says. "You try

A new Festivus ritual

to throw the washers in the hole, and apparently the more you drink the better you get at it."

The game of pitching washers and Festivus share similar homespun roots. It's not surprising they found each other. In its literature, the International Association of Washer Players (IAWP) suggests the game likely started with a backyard wager that went something like: "Betcha I can toss this here washer into that oil can over yonder."

Here Are the Basic IAWP Rules for Pitching Washers

(A complete set, along with tips on strategy, is available at www.washers.org.)

If possible, use 2.5-inch-diameter washers.

Generally, there should be two holes in the ground, each about 4 inches in diameter and 4.5 inches in depth, 25 feet apart with players facing one another. Players must pitch from within one stride of the hole on their side.

Each player's turn consists of pitching two washers at the opposite hole. A washer in the hole (called "a cupper") counts for 5 points unless an opponent also holes one, in which case the cupper is considered "capped" and is canceled out.

After each round, if no one has scored 5 points, the washer closest to the hole counts for one point.

First team to 21 wins: 11-0 is a skunk.

FESTIVUS FRISBEE GOLF

In the spirit of travel to Gorzex, Festivus for Greg Johnson is all about flying saucers—of a sort. Because disc golf uses poles as targets instead of holes as in regular golf, it occurred to Greg, a *Seinfeld* fan and treasurer of the Willamette Disc Golf Club, to name the annual local tourna-

Festivus Frisbee golf uses poles as holes

ment he hosts "Festivus." He prints special discs, showing Mary's Peak of the Oregon Coast Range in the background and a pole in the center.

In 2004, tournament co-winners split a $78 prize. "I would have won myself for the Advanced Masters division," Greg, still upset, says, "if not for a *Tin Cup*–style collapse, throwing out of bounds three times in a row on my second-to-last hole." Before the event, there'd been talk that the tourney couldn't end until someone wrestled Greg to the ground. In the end, no one tried. "They figured I was not in the mood after my collapse."

FESTIVUS TRIVIA TEAM

For a group of college students in Stevens Point, Wisconsin, Festivus is celebrated with trivia. The "Festivus for the Rest of Us" group bills itself as "The Hottest Young Trivia Team This Side of the Little Plover River."

FFTROU competes in major regional contests. Generally, these marathon competitions are run by small radio stations, which broadcast questions over the air. Dozens—sometimes hundreds—of teams like FFTROU gather themselves in computer-filled rooms and try to find answers as quickly as possible using any resources they want. The answers are phoned

Trivia team logo

FFTROU celebrates a correct answer with a victory dance

in to the radio station and after fifty or so straight hours of trivia, the team with the highest score wins.

Things can get strange in the pressure cooker of the trivia room at contest time. After taking a bite of a friend's brownie at a 2003 contest, team co-captain Greg Ormes looked up in bliss and asked, "Has the whole world gone delicious?" Later, team member Justin Young wondered aloud, "Did you know we could clean the whole room with duct tape?"

FFTROU's highest finish so far is 29th out of 72 teams at the St. Cloud, Minnesota, TSI: Trivia Scene Investigation contest run by station KVSC 88.1-FM. During hour 13 of that contest came one of FFTROU's greatest moments, a complete guess that turned out to be correct. "A Festivus Miracle," Greg says.

> QUESTION: In the television series *Kablam!* during the segment "Life with Loopy" there was a skit called "2000 Leagues Under the Sofa." What did level 94 feature?
> ANSWER: Jimmy Hoffa.

Festivus Mating Rituals

The AOG, the FOS—enough rituals for some, but for others, a party's not a party unless there's booty-chasing. That's why these Festivus innovators have added activities to set the libido panting.

Festivus can sometimes get complicated

KISS YOUR EX-LOVER

Bob and Jane and Ted and Lise have had about as many romantic entanglements with one another as a group of four can have. Most of the year, the 50-something-year-olds live separate lives, but come Festivus, which for them flits between January and February depending on the friends' schedules, everyone heads to Lise's apartment in Binghamton, New York, and the old sparks fly.

"Tom and Bob still lust after Lise," says Jane Harrow, a retired schoolteacher and, according to her, the most chaste of the bunch.

There must be some magic in that old aluminum banister Jane drags over each year and plunks into a Christmas tree stand. In the middle of winter, passions of springtimes past blossom anew. "Lise is extremely vain and extremely good-looking," Jane says. "We take group photos, always one with Bob kissing Lise."

The four soldier on, ignoring the month and the years of the calendar, hewing to their invented take on the invented holiday. They sing "O Festivus" to the tune of "O Christmas Tree," adding the lyrics, "for the rest of us." They eat macaroons. Last year Tom gave Jane a gift, a DVD of *Saturday Night Live*. She doesn't have a DVD player. She complained at his thoughtlessness. He accepted that he was a disappointment. By midnight it was over. As can happen when salad days have passed, nothing went beyond the kissing and everyone slept snug in separate beds.

EROTIC PERFORMANCES

Enter the Alwun House, a nonprofit art space in Phoenix,

Arizona, for the February 2005 edition of the annual Erotic Poetry and Music Festivus and be greeted by three women dressed as Playboy bunnies with bright pink hair.

Promising. Continue into a large bottom-floor room and find performers beating tambourines, stroking guitars, and reading sixteenth-century erotic poetry in a show called "Mystic Rapture."

Flit to another gallery, where it's best to avoid getting too close to the Ritual Fire dancers. They are smeared with flammable gel that titillates them as they play erotically for a transfixed audience.

The art includes a man with his hand in a sock that he argues with as if it's an unruly part of the male anatomy. It is an old fight that many have had before. Can love follow lust or must the order be reversed?

This is not *Seinfeld*'s Festivus, explains Kim Moody, director of the Alwun House. This Valentine's-season Festivus harkens from the holiday's original inventors. "I always liked ancient Rome," Moody says. "It might have something to do with the men running around in black leather thongs."

Above the bar, a troupe of fifteen Kama Sutra dancers called "Of the Earth" writhe.

"To me," Moody concludes, "the word 'Festivus' means 'refined hedonism.'"

MISS FESTIVUS

"I felt very important," Julie Manker of Pleasant Plains, Illinois, says of the moment when the Miss Festivus sash, cobbled together from newspaper clippings and oddly shaped letters, was laid across her shoulders at a Festivus

Julie Manker in all her glory

bash in Springfield, Illinois, on December 18, 2004, also the day of her 30th birthday.

It's true there weren't actually any other contestants. Julie simply decided she was Miss Festivus and crowned herself—a nonconformist criteria she suggests all future Miss Festivuses follow.

As a model for future queens, Julie stands tall.

When she was just 20 months old, Julie was already earning celebrity status. She was written up in a local bowling magazine as the youngest bowler ever in Illinois.

"My father owned three bowling alleys," the bespectacled Julie, ever not-demure, says.

After she broke her leg playing volleyball on a scholarship to Butler University, doctors said Julie would have trouble playing any sport again. The future Miss Festivus scoffed at the diagnosis. She headed to Winter Park, Colorado, to take up snowboarding.

Before long, she was bored with living the life of a shred-betty: by day flying over death-defying snow jumps and by night talking about flying over death-defying snow jumps. She set out to find a new challenge.

The Springfield Fire Department was looking for a few good women, and Julie took their test. She dragged dummies, worked hoses, flaunted her skill at mouth-to-mouth, and aced it.

The department hasn't yet had an opening for her, so in the meantime she works as a high school technology teacher. Miss Festivus also helps out her boyfriend, Chris Nickell, editor in chief of *Impala SScene,* a magazine for people involved in souping up and racing 1994–1996 Chevrolet Impala SS and other GM B-Body models.

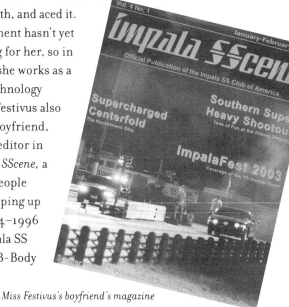

Miss Festivus's boyfriend's magazine

Suggested Categories for Judging a Miss Festivus Contest

by Chris Nickell, boyfriend of Julie Manker, the original Miss Festivus

- How she looks laying down in the backseat of an Impala
- Bowling talent (in the 170 neighborhood is nice)
- Mechanical bull riding aptitude
- How shapely she appears in a firefighter's outfit
- Experience serving in pit crew at drag races
- Ability to fashion her own Miss Festivus sash

Miss Festivus drags a dummy

Miss Festivus at 20 months

Julie comes from a family of beauty pageant winners. Her sister was Miss Fourth of July in Jacksonville, Illinois, in the 1960s, and her niece won Miss Greene County in 1993.

But unlike her forebears, who had to parade their bodies and flaunt their personalities in front of judges to win top honors, Julie decided for herself she was a queen.

Using these un-rules, there need be no *wannabe* Miss Festivuses. Anyone who feels deserving can buy a sash and crown herself.

"It's about being well-rounded," Julie advises future queens. "You're not just stuck inside the box, you have to try new things and be adventurous."

Spontaneous Festivi

They didn't know they were having Festivus in Frankenmuth, Michigan, until they were halfway through it.

One night in December 2001 Elizabeth Zill's teenage daughter Kelty was whining about the family not having a Christmas tree. She had reason to whine—there were trees all around. In fact, Frankenmuth, population 4,838, is home to Bronner's CHRISTmas Wonderland, which claims to be the largest Christmas store in the world. Bronner's, which is across the street from the Zill house, carries more than 150 different types of nutcrackers and sells 1.3 million glass ornaments a year. The store has billboards as far away as Florida, and two million people visit annually.

Elizabeth was sick of Frankenmuth dolling itself up for Christmas. "They start before Halloween," she gripes. Nor was she was in the mood to shell out $40 for a tree just to please Kelty.

The Zill holiday feast was a fend-for-yourself deal from whatever could be found in the fridge. There was tension. Staring. Grievances about "cheapness." Countergrievances about how some people could benefit from seeing the wisdom of "thriftiness." Amanda Morse, Elizabeth's other daughter, had traveled to the house with her husband and 2-year-old son. The tot started wrestling with a squeeze toy.

It was like an undeclared Festivus was happening.

Kelty kept whining. And then it struck Elizabeth like a frying pan to the noggin, something she'd seen on TV once.

She rushed onto the back porch, grabbed an empty coatrack that had been standing there, dragged it into the living room, and told Kelty, "'This is your Festivus pole. Enjoy it,'" Elizabeth recalls. "Oh my gosh, Kelty didn't see the humor in it."

"The rest of us were in tears we were laughing so hard."

But soon the tension popped and disappeared like a pine needle in a living room fire. Elizabeth strung some lights around the coatrack. A pile of presents formed under it.

Across the street, a permanent seventeen-foot-tall statue of Santa Claus stared at the Zill home from atop one of the three fake mountains of dirt Bronner's had built to simulate alps in Frankenmuth.

"It wears on you after a while," Amanda says. "That coatrack made me immensely happy."

Elizabeth remembers the accidental Festivus fondly, too. "We're warped," she says.

Festivus Yes, Fake Snow No! A Tale of a Cold Festivus at the Office

by Sarah Garland, former staff reporter at a community newspaper

I hated my boss, my coworkers, and my job as a re-porter at a weekly newspaper in Queens, New York. More than anything, I hated that the cheap bastards wouldn't install heat vents in my back office.

Every morning I settled into my desk in the editorial department without removing my hat and scarf. I exchanged my coat for a ragged, grandpa-style sweater and slipped on a pair of gloves with the fingers cut off for typing. With high-pitched Long Island accents, the ladies from sales would occasionally come back to our frigid office lamenting that the lack of heat forced me to dress like a homelss person.

Right at the moment when a well-sharpened pencil plunged into my boss's aorta was a tempting scenario despite the potential jail time, Festivus came to save me.

A day after Thanksgiving the publisher of the news-paper—a vision in a pastel fur hat and heavy jewels—sailed through the door to announce the commencement of the annual Holiday Decoration Contest.

The salesladies went to work. Soon, twinkling lights, fake snow, and tinsel waved in the stuffy air flowing from the heat vents up front, and I was inspired.

Under a poinsettia that, in the bitter backroom cold, had turned brown and dropped its leaves into a pile none of the reporters bothered to pick up, I taped up a sign in red marker: "Happy Festivus." Smiles twitched on the faces of the other downtrodden editorial staff. Pictures of the Grinch and Scrooge McDuck were soon tacked up on bulletin boards.

When we were scolded and ordered to take down our decorations, the spirit of Festivus only took stronger hold in my heart. I aired my grievances at my boss, telling her she was stingy and journalistically corrupt. I quit and have been happily freelance-writing, somewhat warm, and relatively grievance-free ever since.

Dad Doug and son Elian Rubin raise the pole in Princeton, New Jersey. "Festivus makes sense," Doug says.

Festivus at the Office

The need for office workers to enjoy at least one evening a year in which they drink together, complain overly loudly about their superiors, and drunkenly make good on a year's worth of flirtatiousness by kissing sloppily behind the photocopier will likely continue to necessitate the annual office "holiday" party. What has caused problems in recent years is deciding what to name the party and how to decorate for it. The requirement of complete tolerance of *all* religions—including *no* religion—in the workplace has ruled out even the potential triple-inclusiveness of a Hanu-Christma-Kwanzaa party.

Enter Festivus. Devoid of religious connection and yet somehow affiliated with the idea of celebrating something or another, Festivus is the perfect nothing that avoids excluding anyone. Plus, it comes with a cheap decorating scheme: Buy a pole, make it stand up, and the party is good to go.

"You know how places are," says Tatiana Hinosotis, who, as social chair of the Student Engineering Council at the University of Texas at Austin, threw a successful Festivus-themed banquet complete with Grievance Airing and a pole. "They don't like things with religious connotations."

Best of all, for many employers, supervisors, and insurers, a Festivus party does without that most feared of all potential sexual-harassment magnets: the office mistletoe.

The Songs of Festivus

Music

Some Festivus songs, like Festivus parties, are fully realized. Some are mere fragments scrawled in matchbooks and graffitied on bathroom stalls. Here is a sampling of all types.

GATHER 'ROUND THE POLE

Adam Park, the Los Angeles, California–based movie producer who wrote this song, believes it will become the "Jingle Bells" of Festivus.

Gather 'Round the Pole

© Adam Park

moderate folk tempo

Back in eigh teen four ty-four   The Fes ti vus snail was heard to roar.

That ol' snail sure caused a fuss.   His roar brought us Fes ti vus.

chorus
Ga ther 'round the pole, young wi shers.   Ga ther 'round to toss your wa shers.

Ga ther 'round the rest of us.   The time has come for Fes ti vus!

Back in eighteen forty-four
The Festivus snail was heard to roar.
That ol' snail sure caused a fuss.
His roar brought us Festivus.

CHORUS:
Gather 'round the pole, young wishers.
Gather 'round to toss your washers.
Gather 'round the rest of us.
The Time has come for Festivus.

Of Festivus snail they still are talking,
'Cause Papa Dan one day went walking
Among the hills of old upstate,
Where he found that shell so great.

On the shell was a hieroglyphic
Of a source quite unspecific.
Papa Dan shook to his core.
He blew that shell and heard its roar.

CHORUS

That roar spread across the land.
Silver poles began to stand,
And the people who'd been abstaining
Opened up and began complaining.

He took it home to little Dan,
Who wanted to be like his old man.
When little Dan heard its mighty roar,
He wrestled his dad right to the floor!

CHORUS

MISS FESTIVUS PROCESSIONAL SONG

A newly crowned queen deserves a song. Here's one that makes sure Miss Festivus gets what she deserves.

Miss Festivus Processional Song

© Shakes Juliet

somewhat stately

| C | C | G7 | C |

There she is, Miss Fes ti vus. She's rel a tive ly un- ven e mous. She

| C | C | dm | G7 | C |

makes us swoon, She's no ba boon. She is Miss Fes ti vus!

2) She's everthing we wish we were,
Some extra flesh, that's for sure.
But we don't mind,
We love that behind.
She is Miss Festivus!

3) Four eyed one, high school was cruel,
They never saw your inner jewel.
But that was bull.
You're beautiful,
You are Miss Festivus!

em/G am/G A7/G G

Interlude: (Here announcer extolls the specific virtues of the newly crowned Miss Festivus.
For example:)
She onced kissed the drummer for the Lemonheads!
She came very close to doing well on her MCAT!
For some reason she calls pants "trousers"!
For a female, she's reasonably proficient at barbeque!

4) Wear your crown, wield your power,
Complain at will, this is your hour.
We know your end,
A new boyfriend.
You are Miss Festivus!

There she is, Miss Festivus.

She's relatively un-venemous.

She makes us swoon,

She's no baboon
She is Miss Festivus!

She's everything we wish we were.
Some extra flesh, that's for sure.
But we don't mind,
We love that behind.
She is Miss Festivus!

Four-eyed one, high school was cruel,
They never saw your inner jewel.
But that was bull.
You're beautiful,
You are Miss Festivus!

INTERLUDE:
(Here announcer extolls the specific virtues of the newly
crowned Miss Festivus. For example:)
She once kissed the drummer for the Lemonheads!
She came very close to doing well on her MCAT!
For some reason she calls pants "trousers"!
For a female, she's reasonably proficient at barbecue!

(back to verses)

Wear your crown, wield your power,
Complain at will, this is your hour.
We know your end,
A new boyfriend.
You are Miss Festivus!

SO GOOD YOU DO NOT SMELL

Sung to the tune of "Waiting Around to Die" by Townes
Van Zandt:

Father Festivus
Please don't come this year
You used to be so down
With your refusal of fake cheer
And your one cauliflower ear
But Festivus can do without you
Now you lousy clown

We said no tinsel
Is that hard to get?
But you would not be swell
You really are a piece of dirt

Festivus songs around the campfire

So good you do not smell
No
So good you do not smell

FESTIVUS DRINKING SONG

Repeat many times to any tune ("Pop Goes the Weasel" works). Start each round with "carrot cake" and before each new verse the next person in line shouts out a new food item to be sung. If the next person cannot come up with a food item quickly, he or she "loses." If one of the members of the rest of the group cannot remember the new food item while singing the verse, that person "loses." Sing faster with each verse.

Festivus we bait you
Festivus we berate you
Old carrot cake in the back of the fridge
We wish we hadn't a ate you

"BABAGANOUSH!"

Festivus we bait you
Festivus we berate you
Old babaganoush in the back of the fridge
We wish we hadn't a ate you

"MINIATURE RACLETTE PICKLES!" (making the food item as ridiculous as possible is good strategy)

Festivus we bait you
Festivus we berate you
Old miniature raclette pickles in the back of the fridge
We wish we hadn't a ate you
(etcetera)

THE FESTIV-US FESTIVAL

The promoter of a showcase of underground music in Edmonton, Alberta, decided Festivus was the perfect name to slap on the event. It started as the working title and stuck, explains Jay Cairns. The homage to the holiday didn't go as far as acquiring a pole. "We didn't," says Cairns, "have the stick or whatever."

THE SONGS OF FESTIVUS

O FESTIVUS!

Joe, a member of the Texas National Guard who asked that his last name not be printed, was at a December 23 Festivus party in Dallas when the beer ran dry. "Not a lot of our girlfriends came," Joe says. "They thought it was silly the same way women think the Three Stooges is silly as opposed to high art."

The group headed to a downtown bar called Dick's Last Resort. "We had heard there was going to be some Festivus-celebrating there," Joe says.

Boy, was there. "A group of six at a table were belting out this Festivus song to the tune of 'O Canada!'" Joe says. "No one could give me a coherent answer about who wrote it or when or how." Ever resourceful, the military man scrawled the lyrics down on a scrap of paper.

"I've hummed it in the car, but I haven't performed it since and I probably won't until next December 23."

A disciplined man. Here is what Joe took down. Sing to the tune of "O Canada!"

O Festivus!
Our humble holiday.
Serenity Now is our only goal today.

With glowing hearts we see thy shining pole,
No tinsel there to distract our souls!

From far and wide,
O Festivus, to air grievances we're free.

Thy feats of strength are glorious to me.
Frank Costanza, we tip our hat to thee.

O Festivus, we'll pin you first, you'll see.

107

Beyond the
Festivus Party

Manifestations of Festivus

Festivus lives. It is part of the conversation. Its nothingness has come to mean something.

What is that something? Well, people have started naming cats "Festivus," if that means anything. Evangelical Christians in North Carolina have tried recruiting the young by calling their Christmas parties Festivus parties. Does that mean anything?

How about the fact that for two years Ben & Jerry's produced a Festivus flavor of ice cream? Or that someone in Florida installed a Festivus sign next to a nativity scene on the lawn of a government building as a protest? Or that Festivus is the name of a National Football League quarterback's regimen?

Religion, commerce, sports, politics, pets—it must mean something, right?

THE FESTIVUS HOUSE

It's Festivus 365 days a year at the Festivus House, a two-story structure with the word permanently mounted across its front, shared by four students at Miami University of Ohio.

As one might imagine, there are hijinx galore.

"One time some raw meat fell out of the freezer," says res-

The substance spilled on the steps of the Festivus House at
Miami University was not identifiable

ident Tyler Mecham, 21, a senior accounting major. "At the end of the night I was really drunk and picked it up and threw it against the wall as hard as I could and for the whole next day we had hardened raw meat on the wall."

There is a tradition at Miami, located in Oxford, Ohio, of students naming their houses, usually using puns and references to activities undergraduates find important: Genital Hospital, Boot 'n' Rally, and Octopussy are three recent house names.

"Festivus" was born of a desire to be different. Execution was cheap. "We got some plywood, painted it with spray paint in the colors," says housemate Josh Fawley, 21, pausing his video football game to chat with a visitor. "Then Joe went up into the attic and we tied some rope to the sign and he pulled it up. It was an adventure."

"We had a Festivus pole out front," Josh continues, nodding toward the front door from his perch on a black leather sofa. "It was stuck in the ground. It blew over."

No one has stuck it back in the ground. Likewise, the lads strung lights on the Festivus sign for a party in the spring, but the "F" blinked out soon after and hasn't been fixed. "Fixing the 'F' will be tough," Tyler says. "There's a bees' nest up there."

A typical day in the Festivus House might start with Tyler feeding his phosphorescent fish Ray Ray and Georgia. "They glow under a black light," he boasts.

Later, Tyler and Joe will pick up their guitars and practice the songs "Chasing Amnesia" and "Better When You're Gone" that they play in their band named Bell. Nighttime will find Joe lying on his single bed with a plaid bedspread on it, staring at a poster of two young women in white jeans. "He found that poster," Josh says. "We don't know who the girls are."

Festivus miracles don't always come when wished for in the rickety white-shingled house on East Sycamore Street.

"One time," Tyler says, "we shot the fire extinguishers off all around the house, but we had to leave the house because then you couldn't breathe."

Although the men of Festivus House feel a rush of pride on those almost daily occasions when someone rolls down a window and shouts "Happy Festivus!" while driving past, they find some of the comments of passersby confusing.

"It's weird," Tyler says during a break in studying. "I was walking down the sidewalk near the house the other day and I heard someone say, 'I'd rather live in the dorm next year than that sh——hole Festivus. It has to be the worst house on campus.'" Tyler pauses. "We must have had a bunch of trash out. I don't know."

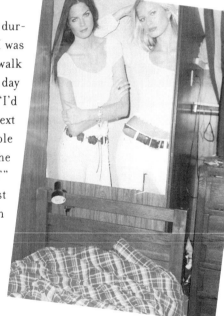

Where Joe dreams

Josh

Georgia is the one on top—or maybe that's Ray Ray

Festivus House bathroom

FESTIVITIS

Brett Fischer, a physical trainer whose facility in Phoenix attracts NFL and Major League Baseball players in the off-season, named the brutal 25- to 30-minute circuit of running and twisting exercises he sets up every Friday "Festivus." "The word has taken on a new meaning," Brett explains. "It's a conglomeration of a workout regiment, a festival-like attitude, and *Seinfeld* thrown in."

The workout, consisting of a series of 5- to 6-second Feats of Strength, is tough. "Some guys have puked," Brett says.

Festivitis

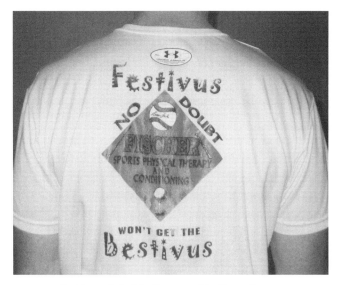

T-shirt made by Jake Plummer of the Denver Broncos

With such a reputation, many athletes choose to skip Fridays at Fischer Sports. Brett invented a word for the disease of not showing up Fridays: "Festivitis."

Those who refuse to come down with a case of it include Jake Plummer, the quarterback of the Denver Broncos. He showed up one Friday with T-shirts he'd had printed that he gave to anyone who completed the course. The T-shirts read, "Festivus Won't Get the Bestivus."

FESTIVUS FELINES
Festivus has become a popular cat name. Here are the stories of Festivus, Microfestivus, and Festy, each told by their owners.

115

The Happy Tale of Festivus
(with some magic realism at the end)

by Brittany Benson, an eighth grader from Fincastle, Virginia

"Oh, Mommy, let's get that one," my little sister said, pointing.

"What do you think, Brittany?" my mom asked.

I took her from my mom. There was something strange about her. It wasn't really her looks; there was just a strange thing about her. I loved it.

"I love her," I said. "She is the coolest!"

"All right, we'll take her," my mom said.

We all started trying to think of a name. Finally, my mom said, "How about Festivus?" It fit her. A strange name for a strange holiday and now for a strange cat.

When we got home, we all wrestled with her a bit, and then it was time for bed. Festivus was obviously not ready for bed. She kept attacking my fingers.

Festivus

Two weeks later, I was watching TV when I heard the top part of "Heart and Soul" being played on the piano. The rest of my family had gone to Grandma's, so I got really nervous. When the tune changed to "Ode to Joy" I realized that if it was a robber or someone else bad, they wouldn't be letting me know that they were there.

I crept to the den. I jumped into the room. I was stunned. Festivus was on the piano.

She jumped off and went out the window. The last I heard of her, she was in Orlando, entertaining tourists in Disney World.

The Sad Tale of Microfestivus
by Brittany's mom, Cathy Benson

Microfestivus, daughter of Festivus, came into the world on Memorial Day weekend 2001. Festivus was not a very good mother, much too young to be a mom and so fat already that we knew not her pregnant state until we found a kitten in the dog crate.

I am sad to say that Brittany and I took better care of the kitten than Festivus did. Festivus would yowl to the tiny kitty and Microfestivus would run to her only to be wrestled and boxed by her mother. Alas, Micro never got over her mother's rejection and became always the rebel. Perhaps Microfestivus was doomed from the start trying to live up to her name and her mother's giant shadow. She was a long-haired tortie cat with a dainty face and sweet nature. We never knew who the father was.

Microfestivus met her demise on the road below

our home when the milk truck—a tanker with a semi pulling it—knocked her off in spring 2004 on the way to our neighbor's dairy farm. She knew no boundaries and her complaint with the milk truck was her downfall. You cannot wrestle with a big rig pulling a tanker down a winding country road. May she rest in peace.

The Indifferent Tale of Festy

by Scott Kirschner of Norwalk, Connecticut

We adopted Festy, a feral cat, January 1, 2002, along with her brother Plato. She is fluffy. Her full name was Festivus, which had come from the *Seinfeld* show, and we're big fans, so we kept it. But we call her "Festy." Plato had a dumb name before: Hiccup. It was really affecting his self-worth.

Festy

Although Festy is a dainty little princess, she can be aggressive and pick fights with her brother. One of their favorite games is "Kitty NASCAR," where they run and chase each other from one floor, down the front stairs, across the lower floor, then up the back stairs over and over.

Although the cats are mostly indoors and don't hunt, my girlfriend thinks Festy would be the better hunter.

Festy is also an addict. She is addicted to Pounce, a cat treat. We're trying to wean her, but the withdrawls are ugly.

The Exploitation of Festivus

As if it's not enough that there are now two books about Festivus (*Festivus: The Holiday for the Rest of Us*, Warner Books, 2005, Hachette Audio, 2006, expanded paperback edition, Grand Central Publishing, 2008; and *The Real Festivus*, Perigree, 2005), businessmen and others have schemed how to milk the holiday in myriad other ways. That this would infect it with the one element that most attracts many Festivus followers by its absence, commercialism, seems not to be a concern of those who would use Festivus for their own ends.

"We had a flash animation

In the flavor graveyard since 2002. Time for a revival?

Charity

WHAT: Festivus Maximus, concert to benefit Autism Society of Greater Cincinnati, held at Southgate House, Newport, Kentucky, December 18, 2004.
BRAINCHILD OF: David Storm, musician and father of autistic son.
PLEASE EXPLAIN: "We are trying to associate autism with something other than Dustin Hoffman and *Rain Man*."
RAISED: $2,000.

WHAT: The Drive for Rebecca, a foundation for children with autism, declared itself "The Unofficial Sponsor of Festivus" in an online appeal.
BRAINCHILD OF: Jonathan Singer, father of Rebecca.
PLEASE EXPLAIN: "What does *Festivus* have to do with autism? Absolutely nothing."
RAISED: During December 2004, the foundation's Festivus Web site page garnered 156 hits, but Singer does not know how much of the over $200,000 raised over the drive's two years is due to Festivus.

WHAT: Festivus Food and Beverage Gala, Calgary, Alberta, to benefit Children's Wish Foundation of Canada, November 2004 and 2005.
BRAINCHILD OF: Mark Kondrat and Bill Robinson, sponsors.

PLEASE EXPLAIN: "We were going to call it Christmas around the World. We decided a few months before-hand we wanted a catchier name."
RAISED: $8,500.

WHAT: Festivus Pole outside office of University of Texas at Austin's Student Engineering Council winter 2004 to benefit a family from the Founation of the Homeless.
BRAINCHILD OF: Tatiana Hinosotis, SEC social chair.
PLEASE EXPLAIN: "[We put] a pole outside of the office with gift tags decorated with what the family wanted."
RAISED: Around $400 in cash and gifts.

WHAT: Entrance fee to University of Dalhousie Psychology Department End of Exams Festivus Party was a nonperishable food item for the local food pantry.
BRAINCHILD OF: Sara King, doctoral student.
PLEASE EXPLAIN: "We usually just get really hammered, that's pretty much what it is."
RAISED: a pretty big pile of soup.

WHAT: Fifth Annual Festivus Fundraiser to benefit AIDS research, held at the Urban Living Center in Kansas City, MO, April 26, 2008, and featuring costumed thumb-wrestling.
BRAINCHILD OF: Julianne Donovan, graphic designer
PLEASE EXPLAIN: "Less talk and more wrestling!"
RAISED: $500.00

on our Web site where a gingerbread man came out and plugged in a Christmas tree and he got electrocuted and then the branches all fell out and it became a Festivus pole," says Dave Stever, director of marketing for Ben & Jerry's. The company produced a Fesstivus-flavor ice cream in 2000 and 2001. The flavor featured broken gingerbread men, brown sugar, and cinnamon.

"We were trying to get at the essence of what it would be," he says.

Not everyone went along with the marketing plan.

In 2000, Joyce Millman railed in *Salon* against the flavor. "Weren't those ice-cream makers listening when Frank set down the basic tenets of Festivus?" Millman wrote. "Nor commercialism. No frills. *No tinsel*."

The ultimate failure of Festivus ice cream, like the tempests caused by Festivus beer, may have been due to a backlash against the attempt to distill the essence of something undistillable.

Or it may have been that ice-cream aficionados thought the flavor tasted like sawdust and burnt telephones. Whatever the case, the flavor sold out its 65,000-gallon initial run, but not at what Ben & Jerry's considered a high enough "velocity." Festivus was sent to the flavor graveyard.

There is a petition at the Web site ipetitions.com asking the company to bring it back. "Few ice cream flavors have approached Ben & Jerry's Festivus in terms of overall harmonious flavor composition," the petition notes. Emily Gillespie of Ohio, signatory number 110, added, "I love Festivus! I look for it every Christmas/holiday season!

"Oh, please, please, please!" Juan Carlos Guerrero, number 91, wrote. "Damn you B & J's, you gave us a taste of paradise, then you rip it away!"

As of spring 2008, there were 120 signatures. Ben & Jerry's says it has no plans to resurrect Festivus, but the company insists it remains pleased with its whole Festivus experience. "It was successful from a PR standpoint," Stever says, citing statistics that 120 million people in the United States saw news stories about his company's Festivus ice cream.

The stomach is not the only vulnerable point at which would-be Festivus exploiters are attacking. There's also the soul.

Bethany United Methodist Church in Summerville, South Carolina, ran Winter Festivus '04 in a local park in an effort to bring young people closer to the fold. Christian rock music was blasted, a large screen showed lyrics like "Everything that has breath praise the Lord," and hot chocolate and popcorn were served. "The focus was Christ," says Matt Yon, Bethany's youth minister.

Why call it Festivus? "We figured the generation of kids would know what it is," he said. "We're real intentional. Christ doesn't call on us to be complacent."

Yon says the event held four days before Christmas was a success, with students from five local schools participating, and he plans on using the name Festivus in years to come.

Despite the unusual way Yon's church used Festivus, it is possible to look at that approach as being true to the Roman roots of the holiday—when Festivus sometimes referred to

On the theoretical set of Festivus—The Movie

the extraordinary way the lower classes behaved on officially sanctioned religious holidays.

Indeed, not all exploitations need be untrue to Festivus. It could be that the best possible outcome for legions of Festivus fans would be a Festivus movie that would some-how capture the uncapturability of the holiday and present it in a fun way.

Something like the following, perhaps?

Festivus—The Movie

A TREATMENT

by Douglas Salkin and Allen Salkin

It's the holiday season. We are in a department store. There are decorations everywhere—candy canes, dreidels, Happy Diwali signs—and holiday music is playing. We see a man, RODNEY THOMAS, striding through the store. He is blocked at every turn by people grabbing clothes and toys and toasters and standing in lines. Rodney is dragging his 5-year-old son, Bobby. The boy looks entranced as he passes the line to see Santa. Bobby and his dad are not stopping. They arrive at their destination: the bathroom. But there is a line here, too. As Bobby fights off peeing in his pants, his father rants about the crowds, the prices, the stupidity he sees in the world. Young Bobby hears this and his little heart shrinks as cynicism starts its infection.

Bobby is never able to find joy during the holidays again. As he grows older we see him staring off into space as his sister tears open her presents. He ignores a girl standing under mistletoe when he is 13. And finally we come to the present day. Bobby is arriving at college on his first day of freshman year.

He is repelled by the conformity. The parties are just like high school with more alcohol. At a dorm-wide holiday party, he stops at a small area on a wall where there's a Happy Kwanzaa sign with a small tusk stapled to it next to an electric menorah stapled

ALLEN SALKIN

to the wall and then a bumper sticker that reads, "Honk if you love Allah!" An African-American female student, someone in a fez, and a guy with curly hair are staring at these displays while behind them two blond-haired dorm mothers are confiding to each other in whispers, "I couldn't figure out what Muslims call Christmas." Over the whole display is a banner that reads "Happy Chrismukwandiwallah!"

As everyone is making plans for winter vacation, Bobby is at a loss. He gets in his car and heads west. After a long drive, annoying holiday songs on the radio, he stops at a roadside diner. He meets a young woman, SCARLETT ROBINSON, who is sitting alone in a booth dressed in a Scarlett O'Hara costume. She just ran away from her fiancé at an office holiday costume party. Bobby gives her a ride. At a rest stop they see what looks like a grizzly bear handcuffed to a tetherball pole. It turns out to be a man, FLORIDA LEE, in a bear suit. Florida had been left behind by his old partner, a carnival muscleman who pretended to wrestle a bear. The cuffs cannot be removed from him or the pole, but the pole is dug out and the bear gets in Bobby's car with the pole still attached.

Eventually, the three stop at a bar in a small town. They enter, and it turns out to be a Festivus party. But the guy who was supposed to bring the pole had failed to show up with one and everyone was depressed. The tetherball pole is a welcome sight. Someone has a hacksaw and frees Florida. Bobby

126

has never seen a holiday party as great as this. They air grievances—Bobby tells the bear his fur smells bad. They wrestle. Scarlett says she's sick of Scarlett jokes and she hates her fiancé for making her wear that stupid costume. She phones him and tells him so. She kisses Bobby.

Back at school, Bobby starts a Festivus club and the movement grows like crazy. He becomes the King of Festivus. Things are great. Scarlett is the Queen. But as the mainstream gets wind of the holiday, commercialization starts to take hold: TV specials, ice-cream flavors, mentions on *Jeopardy!*, a hit song, a movie, a BOOK.

Bobby becomes disillusioned by all of this. He believes in the inexplicable magic of Festivus. He sees that the world is using it as a fad and will toss Festivus aside like a Cabbage Patch Kid in favor of the next Beanie Baby. He looks for a sign. He stares at a Festivus pole as if it will give him guidance. When nothing happens, he is elated. He knows that the true meaning of Festivus is just this. Nothing.

He goes home to see his family. He proceeds to get ridiculously drunk and wrestles his father to the floor and puts him in a full nelson.

—fin—

No? Well, something like that, anyway.

The War on Festivus

Festivus is being dragged into the ring for the raging public wrestling match over where to draw the line between church and state.

The opening bell sounded December 15, 2004, when the Polk County Commission in Bartow, Florida, did not approve a request to allow religious displays on public property.

That night under the cover of darkness, a renegade group from the First Baptist Church of Bartow placed life-size figures of Mary, Joseph, baby Jesus, and a snowman in a makeshift manger outside the county commission building.

Festivus at the center of a First Amendment controversy in Polk County, Florida

And then, a few days later, a sign reading "Festivus for the Rest of Us—Donated to Polk County by the Seinfeld Fan Club" was erected next to the manger. No members of the supposed club came forwad to take credit.

Howls of protest went up. "This was big," says Jason Geary, a reporter who covered the free-speech flap for the *Ledger* of Lakeland. "It seemed to really polarize people."

Next, 78-year-old Stella Darby put up a sign honoring Zoroaster, an ancient mystic. She allowed a gay rights group to attach their own rainbow-colored sign to hers with the words "All We Want for Christmas Is Equality."

The commission held more hearings. Television cameras showed up.

Johnnie Byrd, a former speaker of the Florida House and legal counsel for the Bartow church, told the cameras, "It seems like Christmas is on trial here today."

Commissioner Bob English, who opposed allowing the manger and other displays to stay, said the county should follow President Bush's example. "[Look at] the White House lawn," English said. "I don't think you'll see a nativity scene."

The commission passed a compromise measure, creating a temporary free-speech zone for anyone who registered their display with the county. Zoroaster and Jesus stayed. Festivus, unclaimed, came down. In March 2005, the commission approved a permanent free-speech zone in a picnic area next to the county courthouse. Displays are required to feature a prominent disclaimer that they are not financed by public funds or endorsed by the county.

The next skirmish in the war broke out a thousand miles north in a suburb of Rochester, New York. The same year the hubbub was happening in Florida, Festivus was at the center of a school-based battle over how public education officials define what is religious.

When his high school did not immediately tear down "Happy Festivus" signs students had posted in the hallways, junior Daniel Gallis wrote an editorial that was printed in the *Rochester Democrat and Chronicle* complaining about selective enforcement of federal church/state guidelines. The following is a revised version.

Festivus Rots Young Minds:
One High School Student Explains Why He Wages
War on the Holiday for the Rest of Us

by Daniel Gallis, class of 2005 Irondequoit High School,

West Irondequoit, New York

Despite the finale of *Seinfeld* airing in 1998, before most of my class graduated from eighth grade, Festivus lives on at my public high school in upstate New York.

In fact, judging from the way the school administration treats it, Festivus seems to hold a place more sacred here than Christmas, Hanukkah, Kwanzaa, or any other "religious" holidays.

A few weeks before winter recess in December 2004, someone or some group posted signs throughout the hallways reminding of the celebration of Festivus on December 23. Pictures of the Festivus pole were printed on the signs with the infamous quote spoken by the fictional television character Frank Costanza, "A Festivus for the rest of us!"

The signs stayed on the walls for weeks until they were taken down during the normal course of winter break cleaning.

That would not have happened with "Merry Christmas" signs, which would have been yanked down immediately. Under school policy, those are forbidden, as are signs believed to promote any religion, because of the U.S. Constitution's laws about the separation of church and state.

As I passed those Festivus signs day after day, my fascination turned to objection. People celebrating Festivus was supposedly okay? What about the feelings of people who celebrate the birth of Jesus, the cultural celebration of Kwanzaa, or the eight-day commemoration of Hanukkah in the spirit of their true meanings? Might they not find this new substitute for their holidays to be blasphemous? A Festivus sign *is* a religious statement: anti-traditional religion.

Festivus is hardly harmless.

Allowing a television show to dictate what holidays a person practices omits the self-discovery period of finding—or choosing not to find—faith in a traditional religion. Society needs to provide space, especially for young people like me, to look to their inner beliefs, not the TV set, for the holidays.

Next year, I want those Festivus signs removed immediately.

Asked for comment on the issue Gallis raised, Irondequoit
High School principal Patrick McCue took pains to distance
his school from any controversy. He said the school follows
well-established U.S. Supreme Court rules about maintaining the separation of church and state. Prayer groups are, for
instance, allowed to post notices about the times and places
of meetings, but are not allowed to proselytize on the signs.
Posters for Christmas, Hanukkah, and the like, Principal
McCue says, are included in the prohibition. "Those are
religious holidays," he says. "Festivus is nothing."

The next major battle erupted to the west in Wisconsin,
the same state scarred by the beer wars of Festivus. For
years the town of Peshtigo had been erecting a nativity display on public property. In 2007, it was noticed by the
Freedom from Religion Foundation, which filed a lawsuit
against the town, charging that it was violating the establishment clause of the First Amendment of the U.S.
Constitution, which reads, "Congress shall make no law
respecting an establishment of religion."

Forty miles south, Green Bay alderman Chad Fradette
noticed the Peshtigo fracas and suggested to Mayor Jim
Schmidt that their city put up a similar display at City Hall.
The nativity went up two weeks before Christmas, and after
gripes from the area's secular and non-Christian commu-
nities, the city opened the area up to displays from other
religions, subject to approval by city leaders on a case-by-
case basis.

Local resident Sean Ryan, a practicing Catholic, was
skeptical of the the politicians' inclusiveness. "I saw it as
disingenuous posturing," he says. Ryan decided to test the

civic boundaries. He sent a petition to the Mayor's office, requesting a Festivus pole be added to City Hall.

The request was denied. Authorities told reporters that Festivus is "pop culture" and not religious. The city placed a moratorium on any additions to the display. When a Wiccan wreath was vandalized, it was removed and not replaced.

Meanwhile, locals who opposed the display of religion on public property adopted Festivus as the face of their movement. "People who lived near the mayor were putting up signs that said 'Festivus for the rest of us,' " Mr. Ryan recalls.

Festivus, the holiday of feats of strength, loves a good fight, and it found a doozy in Green Bay.

National news outlets reported on the fracas, and the Freedom from Religion Foundation filed an additional lawsuit against the city of Green Bay.

"Council President Fradette," the lawsuit charged, "deliberately used his public office to place an inherently Christian symbol prominently on government property at the entrance to City Hall, the principal location of local government, rather than on his private property, precisely in order to antagonize, offend, and challenge those persons who object to the public sponsorship of religious symbols on government property."

Liberty Counsel, an organization associated with Rev. Jerry Falwell, took up Green Bay's defense. The nonprofit organization, which provides pro bono legal assistance for anti-gay marriage and antiabortion causes, has come to the aid of many groups across the country who want to display nativity scenes on public property.

In a press release, Liberty Counsel attacked the Freedom from Religion Foundation as "the most extreme separatist organization in the country, claiming its members consist of atheists and agnostics."

Mathew D. Staver, founder of Liberty Counsel, said in the press release that "the national and state legal holiday called Christmas is not a World Religions Day. It's Christmas Day. Christmas is constitutional."

Without Festivus, the local dispute might never have attracted national media attention, which drew the prominent advocacy groups and their eager lawyers.

"I came to realize that if the media can find an excuse to play *Seinfeld* clips," Ryan said, "they're going to run with a story."

As of spring 2008, the lawsuit was ongoing.

The Future

Will people still be celebrating Festivus in a thousand years?

It is not far-fetched to imagine Festivus as a permanent part of the world's holiday firmament, says Anthony F. Aveni, professor of astronomy and anthropology at Colgate University and the author of *The Book of the Year: A Brief History of Our Seasonal Holidays* (Oxford University Press, 2002). After all, Halloween used to be an obscure festival observed by few, Kwanzaa was invented by an academic in California in the 1960s, and Hanukkah has been reinvented in modern times to include gift-giving. "Even Christmas comes out of a pagan holiday that happened around the solstice," Professor Aveni said.

Despite the professor's approach, there's no need to question the provenance of other holidays to evaluate Festivus's chances of making the fourth millennium, says Alyson Beaton, who contributed a chapter on the growing popularity of Festivus to the book *The Business of Holidays* (Monacelli Press, 2004). While many celebrate Festivus as a reaction to the current state of the old holidays, some love Festivus just for its Festivusness.

"It will stick around," Beaton says. "More and more people are going to treat this like an Oscar party sort of thing, or the Super Bowl, this kind of funny cultural thing they do every year. The holiday is fun and it's sort of ridiculous."

What Beaton and others miss is that Festivus has already proved it can survive for thousands of years. Unlike any other holiday, it waits patiently knowing that if one epoch tires of it, another will, inevitably, discover it again and adapt Festivus for its own uses.

It may be that Festivus in five thousand years will have no aluminum pole and no Airing of Grievances. It may involve dance-a-thons or a contest to see who can club the most mutants or a ritual of downing intelligence-fortifying Gorzexian Grog and inventing new magic tricks. A person named Festivus "Flip" Fliporzorai, named after the holiday by his back-to-nature parents, may be elected president of the Milky Way in 7448.

Festivus has persisted so the evidence is it will persist.

Taking it back to its ancient roots, the word "Festivus," really, means nothing more than "the way people behave at a party." This behavior changes as civilizations change, as the ways humans choose to blow off steam changes. Festivus is always current.

As long as there's something to blow off steam about, there will be Festivus.

Acknowledgments

To the many, many Festivus faithful who contributed tales of Festivus frolics, thank you. And thanks, too, to Jennifer Unter, Stacy McGoldrick, Bob Asprinio, Ellen Santaniello, Lisa Arbetter, Nancy Hass, Bob Roe, Jenny Salkin, Rachel Kempster, Craig Young, Jason Pinter, Ben Greenberg, Jordana Rothman, Michael O'Connell, Mari Okuda, Emi Battaglia, Anna Maria Piluso, Roland Ottewell, Cassie Slane, Jerry Stiller, Gabi Payn, Trip Gabriel, and Allison Silver. Special thanks for research assistance to Sarah Garland.

About the Author

Allen Salkin is an investigative reporter. He has written on subjects ranging from the last true waterbed salesman in the San Francisco Bay area to corruption in the Brooklyn courts for the *New York Times*, the *Atlantic Monthly*, the *Village Voice*, *Details*, and other publications.

Allen has been a rubber ducky salesman in Las Vegas, a farm laborer in Crete, a casting agent in Hong Kong, a hotel maid in Venice, a busker in Melbourne, a stand-up comedian in New York, a cafeteria cashier in Squaw Valley, a slacker in San Francisco, and a chocolate chip cookie maker in Waikiki.

For Festivus songs, home movies, and to share Festivus stories, visit www.festivusbook.com.

Photo of Festivus T-shirt on page 115 courtsesy of Brett Fischer.

"The Happy Tale of Festivus" on pages 116–117 by Brittany Benson printed with permission.

Photo of Festivus on page 116 and "The Sad Tale of Microfestivus" on pages 117–118 by Cathy Benson reprinted with permission.

"The Indifferent Tale of Festy" on pages 118–119 and photo on page 118 by Scott Kirschner reprinted with permission.

Photo of Festivus ice cream on page 119 courtesy of Ben & Jerry's Homemade, South Burlington, VT.

"Festivus Rots Young Minds" on pages 130–131 by Daniel Gallis reprinted with permisison of Daniel D. Gallis and the *Democrat and Chronicle*, Rochester, NY.